Questions

The Buddha Way

Questions

A series of explorations by
William Corlett & John Moore

WILLIAM CORLETT
&
JOHN MOORE

The Buddha Way

HAMISH HAMILTON
LONDON

First published in Great Britain 1979 by
Hamish Hamilton Ltd., Garden House, 57–59 Long Acre,
London WC2E 9JZ

ISBN 0 241 10005 4

ACKNOWLEDGEMENTS

The authors and publisher are indebted to the following for the use of copyright material: The Buddhist Society, London, for permission to quote from their edition of *The Dhammapada* (Jack Austin); John Murray, London, for quotations from *The Dhammapada* translated by Narada Thera; Penguin Books, London, for permission to quote from *Buddhist Scriptures* translated by Edward Conze (Penguin Classics © 1959); Charles E. Tuttle & Co. Inc., Tokyo, for permission to quote from *Zen Flesh, Zen Bones* compiled by Paul Reps (Pelican Books edition 1971); Peter Pauper Press, New York, for permission to quote from *Sayings of Buddha* (1957).

Printed in Great Britain by
Ebenezer Baylis and Son Ltd.
The Trinity Press, Worcester, and London

This book is one of a series.

The titles are *The Question of Religion*, *The Christ Story*, *The Hindu Sound*, *The Judaic Law*, *The Buddha Way* and *The Islamic Space*. The books were written in the order as listed, but this in no way implies any suggested precedence of one religion over another, nor any preference on the part of the authors. Each book may be read in its own right, rather as each note of an octave may sound alone.

However, for an octave to be complete, it depends on the developing frequency and character of each note. In the same way, it has been the experience of the authors, approaching this series as one work, to find a similar development as they progressed from one book to another.

The perfect way knows no difficulties
Except that it refuses to make preferences;
Only when freed from hate and love
It reveals itself fully and without disguise;
A tenth of an inch's difference,
And heaven and earth are set apart.
If you wish to see it before your own eyes
Have no fixed thoughts either for or against it . . .

(SENG-TS'AN, *On Believing in Mind*)

One

There is a parable that the Buddha told:

A man travelling across a field encountered a tiger. He fled, the tiger after him. Coming to a precipice, he caught hold of a root of a wild vine and swung himself down over the edge. The tiger sniffed at him from above. Trembling, the man looked down to where, far below, another tiger was waiting to eat him. Only the vine sustained him.

Two mice, one white and one black, little by little started to gnaw away the vine. The man saw a luscious strawberry near him. Grasping the vine with one hand, he plucked the strawberry with the other. How sweet it tasted!

*

We, the authors, are beginning to write a book which we have called "The Buddha Way".

We have elected to start with a story. It is one of a host of similar stories stemming from the Japanese tradition of Zen Buddhism.

Who wrote the story?

What is Zen Buddhism?

Who is the Buddha we have referred to?

What did the story mean to the person who wrote it?

We ask these questions because we want to discover the validity of the story, whether the story-teller knew what he was talking about, and whether we understand what he was trying to say.

But would the answer to any of these questions make any difference to our original reading of the story?

At that moment—when we first read the story—were we not . . .

A* I

simply reading a story? And did not the understanding of that story simply depend upon *our* understanding of it? Perhaps it was pointless; perhaps it was amusing; perhaps it reminded us of something in our own experience; perhaps it put into words something that we recognize but have never considered before.

Perhaps . . .

There are so many stories; every culture has them; every tribe; every family; every person. Stories may be factual (about what has actually happened) or they may be fictitious (about what has not actually happened). The factual stories require accurate memory; the fictitious stories belong to "make-believe", to imagination, to creating through the workings of the mind imaginary events and experiences.

We might therefore summarize by saying that factual stories are "true" and fictitious stories are "untrue" or "false".

But what is this capacity, that we all share, to "imagine"?

Can I imagine something that is totally out of my experience? Can I imagine anything that I do not know?

I imagine: water flowing uphill; no, more than that; a waterfall starting at the base of the cliff and cascading upwards to the summit!

False—not true: but consider, could I imagine thus if I had not already experienced *water flowing*? Could I imagine *water*?

Could you?

What is the *truth* in my imagining? The truth is that water is. What I tell you *about* the water is for you to believe or for you to reject. Because you know what you know *about* water.

However, if I tell you about "feawe" which drips tiny flames enclosed in dew drops and is only found in pockets of space contained in rocks deep in the earth . . . well, you may be fascinated, you may even be prepared to go along with my story . . . but surely you will want to see this remarkable phenomenon for yourself in order to believe it?

Until you see it, you may not name it "false"; but until you see it, will you name it "true"?

2

(By the way, in this example I was trying to "imagine" something totally outside my experience: Fire Earth Air Water Ether . . . FEAWE and should such a phenomenon exist—though doubtless with another name—then I will believe it when I see it!)

And so . . . was there a man who, travelling across a field encountered a tiger? Did he hang from the vine over the precipice? Did two mice, the one white the other black, start to gnaw? And the strawberry? How sweet it tasted. Did it? Only the man can say . . . if he existed.

Can I then not believe what I have not seen or experienced?

Why else do we make a journey?

If there were no new countries to discover, no new sights to be seen, why would we ever set off from where we are now and make the effort to reach the place where we want to be?

In this book we have called the journey "The Buddha Way". It is a journey that we have already begun.

*

No doubt at some time all of us have had occasion to look at a new-born baby.

It lies there peacefully asleep or wide awake . . . gazing, smiling, crying, or murmuring with pleasure . . .

And it may happen that our attention is held by the baby and our minds may become filled with wondering; we may feel that we are face to face with both a mystery and a miracle.

How did the baby come to be?

Oh yes, there are all kinds of explanations which may satisfy the mind's desire for answers. The parents had intercourse, the ovum was fertilized by the sperm, the cells divided and multiplied, the embryo was fed and formed in the womb . . . all kinds of factual explanations. But deep down, underneath those superficial mechanical facts, do we not sense that we do not even begin to comprehend *how* it happened? Are not the explanations simply word descriptions of processes of changing form as observed by man which do not even begin to penetrate the mystery as to how it is done?

3

The *facts* may offer a superficial explanation but the *imagination* is in awe: we cannot imagine, cannot conceive *how* . . .

And perhaps we have also had occasion to look upon someone who has just died?

The body lies there silently dead . . . inanimate, without life, neither asleep nor awake . . . not gazing, not smiling, not crying, nor in pleasure . . .

And there is another miracle, another mystery.

Where did the person go to? And what is this, this body that is left?

Again explanations are offered to satisfy the mind's desire for answers. The breathing has stopped, the heart no longer beats, all the organs of the body have ceased to function, they cannot be revived. The person is dead . . . all kinds of mechanical explanations. But again, deep down, do we not sense that we do not even begin to comprehend *what* has happened? Again, are the explanations not simply word descriptions of processes of changing form as observed by man which do not even begin to penetrate the mystery of what has occurred?

The *facts* may offer a superficial explanation but the imagination is in awe: we cannot imagine, cannot conceive . . .

The dead body that we are looking at was once, presumably, a living being, a person.

And the baby that we are looking at will, all being well, grow into a mature human being, a person.

How?

How does the baby know how to grow into a person?

How does it become an individual and unique adult?

And, finally, how does it know how to die?

Once I was just such a baby myself . . . a small, helpless creature. I can scarcely believe that. How did I become what I am now?

Oh, yes; again there are all kinds of explanations. From what others tell me and from what I remember, I can trace a whole sequence of events that have happened to me since I was a baby—

events that have to a degree moulded what I have turned out to be . . . now.

And no doubt there are all kinds of explanations as yet unknown to me, and a whole sequence of events that will happen to me from this moment which will lead eventually to my death.

Am I then simply the consequence of arbitrary events?

Am I just the product of the reaction of my particular nature with my changing environment throughout the passing years?

Supposing the answer is simply "yes", that still does not explain to me *why I am like I am.*

Did I have any choice in how I started, where I am now or what I will become?

Assuming that I had no say in the original blueprint which dictated the forming of my present character and that I had no say throughout the years of my childhood in what befell me—then in what sense may I consider myself to be other than a haphazard accident?

Of course I have long since come to believe that I am unique, individual, relatively independent and an integrated and consistent person. But in the moment, for example, of contemplating the miracle and the mystery of a new-born baby and wondering how it will become a mature person, am I not challenged to consider what I mean by that?

I was once such a new-born baby; here I am now; how are the two connected? Simply by a sequential chain of accidental events?

Here I am now and one day I will be dead—again a sequential chain of accidental events?

Who am I in this chain?

What can I truly say is me and mine?

I am this person here, now.

How does it come about that I have become aware of myself as a person?

Why do I assume and cling to the idea—or the *fact*—that I am?

I think I know who I am but do I really know?

What is the nature of the essential core of my being, here and

5

now—that which in effect, gives rise to the experience of being me?

Do I like being me?

Having been landed with being me, what am I supposed to do?

Am I just to see my life through as a chapter of accidents and then simply submit to annihilation at death? For surely, as birth gave life, death will take back that life.

What a curious situation we find ourselves in once we begin to scratch the surface of our everyday assumption and concern.

As we hang by the slender vine over the precipice between the twin tigers of destruction and the mice of time begin to gnaw ... what can we do? What are we supposed to do? Is there anything at all left to us, save only that moment of experience?

A thousand questions come bursting like bubbles into the mind ...

*

Just as one would view a bubble, just as one would view a mirage; if a person thus looks upon the world, the King of Death sees him not.

(The DHAMMAPADA)

*

We can, of course, if we so wish, ignore such seemingly explanation-defying questions. It would seem that the majority of human beings do so.

In this book—and in the series to which this book belongs—we the authors are not content to leave it at that. We wish to explore such questions, not so much because we have confidence that we will find the "answers" but because it seems to us a responsibility to do so (*responsibility*: "the ability to respond") as if, for some reason that we may not fully understand, the exploration has to be made for its own sake.

There is evidence enough in the world that men have found reward in such exploration and many have testified that there has been for them no pursuit more worthwhile nor more noble.

Indeed it would seem that the very nature of man's mind requires him to respond thus. Otherwise what possible reason could there be for his having the capacity to consider such questions?

*

If we confine our exploration to a book—we, the authors, to the writing of it, and you, the reader, to the reading of it—will that be enough?

We believe that such an exploration as we are here suggesting should not just be an entertaining enquiry to be picked up and put away again on some bookshelf, to be read when there is time to spare and considered when there is nothing more amusing to do; the questions raised in the mind are a lifetime's pursuit of the highest priority. Ultimately the exploration is the only worthwhile activity possible to man.

Why else are we here?

What else are we here for?

Why were you born?

Why must you die?

Why was I born?

Why must I die?

What is this life that I am living?

Who am I?

*

From the historical record we may surmise that just such questions challenged a man named Siddhartha Gautama about two thousand five hundred years ago. And although the story of his life as handed down to us is acknowledged as being an inextricable mixture of fact and legend, we can assume that he penetrated the mystery and the miracle of human existence to considerable effect because, when he began to expound what he had discovered through years of intensive exploration, he attracted followers and disciples who were so inspired by his teaching that they called him *Buddha*, meaning "Enlightened One".

7

That teaching has since been the inspiration for hundreds of millions of people who have been, and are now, called "Buddhists".

*

As has happened so often throughout history, and naturally so, once an influential teacher dies there arises the desire to perpetuate the inspiration of what he said and did.

Commonly the teaching is initally passed on orally by the teacher's immediate disciples and successors. Then, at a later date, it is set down in writing and propagated further. Gradually, through the passage of time, there come interpreters of the written scriptures and inevitably contention arises as to the validity of one interpretation compared with another. Different schools of thought develop and the original inspiration is transformed. Some of the factions take up stances in direct opposition to others. Such is the way of the world and the evolution of ideas. This is not to suggest that the later developments are invalid; we are simply stressing that it becomes increasingly difficult to be sure of the nature of the original.

However, it would seem sensible for us to be circumspect—for a human tendency creeps into this process which may well be inappropriate and even detrimental. This is the tendency for the various factions to champion their interpretation as the correct one and to accuse the others of being "incorrect".

But incorrect for whom?

You and I may both read the little Zen story with which this chapter begins. I may tell you what it means to me—and you may have quite a different interpretation. Which of us is correct? The story *means* what it *does* to each of us. I would be unwise to discredit your interpretation simply because I don't see it that way. After all, we may both listen to a beautiful piece of music—both of us may be "moved" by it, but neither of us will ever know *how* the other was moved: the experience is uniquely and entirely each his or her own. The only connection is between the music and the individual listener; between the story and the person who reads or hears that story.

Once each of the factions champions its interpretation as the only correct one it is but a short step to the various interpretations becoming formalized and dogmatic and for each faction to promote its interpretation as the one and undeniable truth (an assumption which could only be refuted by the authority of the originator who has long since disappeared—and who may well say: "Here is my gift (the story or the music, the teaching or whatever), here is what I offer you—now it is yours to make of it . . . what you will").

*

Alongside this development—perhaps in an attempt to reach for that which will transcend the contention and discord—the teacher himself tends to become elevated above the fragmentation of his message and becomes increasingly promoted as being himself superhuman. From being respected and revered in his own time as a man of wisdom, he becomes a legend and an image to be worshipped and he may even be accorded "divine" status.

Once worship of the legend has become established, the self-selected "priests" of the tradition introduce ceremony and ritual, chiefly as "memory-aids". According to the persuasiveness of the doctrine and how it feeds the hopes and fears of human society, so greater or lesser numbers of believers are attracted. And, in the course of time, according to the strength of its influence and the number of its adherents, the teaching may become acknowledged as a "religion".

And so today we have a handful of major religions (all of which originated well over a thousand years ago) and a number of minor ones. Many more have died out, some are dwindling remnants, others have been absorbed by more powerful neighbours.

(We should, however, remark that, depending on how we define "religion", there has evolved a major religion over the last century—namely Communism. Already the original teachers such as Marx and Lenin assume superhuman status and images of them are

9

"worshipped" by millions. Whether or not they will eventually be elevated to the ranks of the "divine" is an interesting speculation.)

*

One of the recognized major religions of the world is called Buddhism, a blanket term for varying shades of practice and belief, all of which are derived, more or less tenuously, from the life, words and deeds of a particular man who lived two and a half millennia ago.

The major division of the tradition took place over two thousand years ago and these two factions are called *Mahayana* (Greater Vehicle) and *Theravada* or *Hinayana* (Lesser Vehicle). The former tradition spread northwards from India into Tibet, China, Mongolia and Japan whilst the latter spread southwards and eastwards into Sri Lanka, Burma, Thailand, Cambodia and Laos.

*

Gautama (like, for example, Jesus of Nazareth who lived five or six centuries later) did not apparently attempt to write down his teachings. In fact it seems that he stressed that what he had to say was in response to the needs and circumstances of those around him at the time. (And this emphasis is given by many renowned teachers throughout history and today, presumably because spoken words taken out of their immediate and spontaneous context, especially when written down, are so easily misinterpreted.)

Perhaps we may assume that Gautama knew that inevitably there would be those of his followers who would eventually attempt to record his teaching other than through "living" oral communication. Nevertheless, this was not done apparently until some five hundred years after his death. (By any reckoning, that is a very long time for accuracy of memory to be maintained!)

The scriptures which came to be accepted as the authentic canon of the *Theravada* tradition (known as the "Canon of the School of the Elders") were written down in the Pali language and compiled in

Sri Lanka. This canon is called *Tripitaka* (Three Baskets) and it is a part of it, called *Sutta Pitaka*, which is said to contain records of Gautama's sermons, discourses and sayings. And the most cherished and popular part of this section is called the *Dhammapada* (translated by some as "The Way of Truth") and from which we have already taken a quotation in this chapter.

This *Theravada* tradition contains much material that was evidently intended by Gautama for his immediate disciples, who were expected to lead austere and highly disciplined lives as missionary teachers among the people. Thus it was that some two hundred years after Gautama's death a group of dedicated followers, believing that the teaching was being too conservatively interpreted by the *Theravada* school, began to evolve a more liberal interpretation suitable to the needs of ordinary people, the vast majority of whom could not be expected to undertake the monastic life which the *Theravada* school deemed to be the essential prerequisite for a holy life leading to "enlightenment".

(This fundamental division in Buddhism could be seen as representing the seeds of an extremely provocative debate. To what extent does a man or a woman need a spiritual teacher and to what extent can he or she be expected to discipline himself or herself? To what extent is the self-selected "teacher" or "priest" qualified and privileged, and in what ways?

(These and other questions arising would need a book to themselves. And who could write such a book—the priest or the layman —without being biased!)

This more liberal approach was the inception of the *Mahayana* tradition and its authentic canon was written down in Sanskrit and compiled over a period of several centuries, beginning some seven hundred years after Gautama had died. Like the *Theravada* scriptures, it is divided into three sections, the second of which, called the *Sutras*, contain much the same material as the *Sutta Pitaka*. The third section, called the *Shastras*, is a record of philosophical discourses on the teaching of later teachers. In the course of time, more literature was added and, due to the more secular nature of the *Mahayana*, much of it was of popular appeal in the form of epic stories, poetry and legend.

*

When we further take into account that the two main divisions of Buddhism then sub-divided into many different sects—especially as they were adopted and adapted by the indigenous cultures of the countries to which they spread (one of the most notable of these being the development of Zen Buddhism in Japan), and then that over the centuries hundreds of teachers have emerged and that their interpretations have given rise to thousands of books on the subject—and that all these divisions and sub-divisions, these cultures and interpretations are embraced in the blanket term "Buddhism" . . . then we may well be daunted at the prospect of even beginning to understand what is meant by the Buddhist religion.

But let us ask ourselves a question:

"What is it that we really want to try to do?"

It is the question that we, the authors, have to ask ourselves when embarking upon this short book. It is a question that we must often bring to mind before we come to the last page.

Do we really want to learn *all about* Buddhism?

Do we think that we should spend many years studying all the known scriptures and commentaries of all the different off-shoots in order to arrive at a distillation which we could say was some sort of definitive statement of "Buddhism"?

Even if we did so—and perhaps learned Pali and Sanskrit to help us read the original texts—how could we be really sure that we understood what Gautama had said and meant?

Or do we think that really to gain an understanding of Buddhism —a tradition whose roots are firmly embedded in the East—we ought to go to that part of the world and "become Buddhist"?

Even if we went that far—how could we be sure that we could find a genuine representation of the religion and not just a dead-end branch?

Is there in fact such a thing as genuine Buddhism in the sense that there exists somewhere a teacher or school which the Gautama himself, were he alive, would recognize as truly representing his message?

If nothing was written down for at least five hundred years and it is now two and a half thousand years since the originator himself died, what possible hope is there of ever arriving at a definitive statement as to what the Buddhist religion is?

And, above all, even if there were such an irrefutable and absolutely acceptable definition, what on earth would be the point of it for me, now, here?

So what may we usefully try to do?

It seems to us that there would be no point in attempting to arrive at a definitive answer about what has happened in the past.

It seems to us that the established history, performance and dogma of a particular religion while being perhaps fascinating is nevertheless relatively unimportant. It is just like all other factual information and explanation and like all repetitive and habitual behaviour—like all our yesterdays, perhaps interesting *then*, but only useful in the light of *now*.

The value of a religious tradition must lie in the degree to which it still carries the "spirit" of the original teacher, the degree to which the principles of the message can be distinguished from the plethora of historical interpretation (which may well have been appropriate in its time and place . . . yesterday, somewhere . . .), the degree to which those principles are relevant to now and the degree to which present behaviour may be beneficially governed through response to those principles.

For what would it profit us to try to remember how it felt to be a new-born baby? Far better let us focus our attention on what it really feels like to be . . . now.

In other words, what we can understand of Buddhism is only useful and relevant if it meets a need in us now—if it helps to illuminate the miracle and the mystery and the difficulties of our lives, whoever we are and wherever we happen to be . . . now.

Learning about religion—even adopting and paying lip-service to a particular religion—is little different to learning all about the football scene and becoming a fan of a particular team ... unless in learning about religion we come to understand what it means to *live a religious life* ... which implies, amongst other things, a continuous assessment of *our own* experience, thinking and behaviour in the present.

The man who talks much of the Teaching but does not practise it himself is like a cowman counting others' cattle: he has no part in the Brotherhood. The man who can repeat but little of the Teaching, yet lives it himself, who forsakes craving, hatred and delusion, possesses right knowledge and calmness, clings to nothing in this or any other world, he is a follower of the Blessed One ...

(The DHAMMAPADA)

*

The Buddha Way may start by reading words on a page—even a page such as this—or by seeing a flower, or by feeling a pain ... or by any other experience given to man; but from then on it is a lifetime's journey, and every moment—when we remember—we will have to discipline and modify the way we think and the way we behave.

And the end of the journey?

We will each of us be unable to say anything about that until we reach it, and when we do, perhaps there will be no need then for words?

*

If we do want to learn all about a particular religion called Buddhism (or Christianity, Mohammedanism, Judaism, Hinduism, or whatever) then so be it. There are many, many books that will help us to do so.

But as we have implied in the books in this series, it seems to us more relevant to focus attention on the phenomenon "religion" itself, and then try to see in what ways a particular tradition contributes to, and thus throws light on, what it is that "religion" means.

Thus we could see ecumenicism not as some kind of patched-up amalgamation of different *forms* of religion but as a realization of what it is that trancends all form—the religious "spirit" or inspiration which caused all the religions in the first place.

Religions arise as a *result* of a deep need in the psyche. The performance and perpetuation of the established religions (most of which are now centuries old) is doomed unless they aspire to meet that need *as it manifests today*.

And so, in looking at the phenomenon "religion" we inevitably look to see what that need is.

*

What is that need?

We soon discover that there is no absolute definition in words of that need, for at heart it is a feeling . . . a longing or yearning . . . which is very personal and difficult to express.

Each of us will *feel* the need, or the "lacking" or the "longing", each in his own experience, each in his own way. Therefore each of us must discover, observe and define for ourselves. After all, you cannot observe for me, can you? Nor I for you, can I? In the ultimate analysis it is bound to be "up to you" and "up to me" . . . for I came alone into this world and alone I will depart.

In setting out then to discover the nature and the resolution of the yearning, each may look at any or all of the world's religions and philosophical traditions and see how they may help in the search.

It is not so much that all religions necessarily say the same thing. (Although fundamentally they are all the same in their demonstration of the "inexpressible".) They are all responses to human need and they express themselves in different ways. It is just a matter of finding the particular expression (if any) to which your nature responds; the one which enlightens your need as you experience it.

Today is a stimulating time to live out the search. The present age of global communication means that you do not have to be restricted to the traditional religion(s) of the area in which you were born.

The world is indeed our oyster and the great religious and philosophical traditions our priceless pearls.

Ecumenicism is now a real possibility because we have more and more opportunity (in democratic states at any rate) to draw on the wisdom of all traditions and choose whichever dispensation and discipline speaks to our particular natures.

(A timely reminder, however: This does not mean choosing bits and pieces from here and there just to suit our passing fancies. At some point in development every tradition requires deep commitment.)

*

And so it is from this standpoint that we may take an introductory look at the teaching of Siddhartha Gautama who was called Buddha —"enlightened one"—as it survives and is represented *now*.

Now it does not matter what is supposed to be authentic or non-authentic. *Now* we may consider some of the concepts and principles and see if we can capture something of the "spirit" of a message that has inspired hundreds of millions of people throughout the centuries since it was first spoken.

Here and *now* is where we are, and the only value lies in how our needs may be met . . . here and now.

The legend or the history tells us that Gautama was a man—an ordinary, questioning human being—just as we are ordinary, questioning human beings. What was extraordinary about him was his dedication to the search for the ultimate answers.

The power of the questions is where we begin.

As we have suggested, if we stand back from our everyday concerns and pursuits, we find ourselves confronted by a mystery and a miracle.

Who am I?

How did I come to be what I am?

What am I here for?

What happens when I die?

Such questions did Gautama ask, and through the questions he was led to "enlightenment".

The Buddha proposes "the Way" to penetrate and resolve these questions, for each of us.

The message is not a comfortable one from the worldly point of view; it calls for considerable effort and even sacrifice.

It is up to you, as it is up to me, whether we feel the pursuit is worthwhile. Perhaps by the time we have to make our final commitment—if that time should come—there will be no choice.

Meanwhile. . . .

*

. . . Grasping the vine with one hand, he plucked the strawberry with the other. How sweet it tasted!

Two

A long time ago in China there were two friends, one who played the harp skilfully and one who listened skilfully.

When the one played or sang about a mountain, the other would say: "I can see the mountain before us."

When the one played about water, the listener would exclaim: "Here is the running stream!"

But the listener fell sick and died. The first friend cut the strings of his harp and never played again. Since that time the cutting of harp strings has always been a sign of intimate friendship.

*

If this book remains simply a number of words along a line and a number of lines upon a page and a number of pages between two covers, then we, the authors, and you, the reader, will not be true friends. And yet the *essence* of this book, from the writers' point of view is that we are embarking upon a mutual quest; upon a journey; upon a way.

We have chosen to make this journey because we are not content with the land in which we live. This discontent is neither *good* nor *bad*, it is simply that life seems unfulfilled.

Why should this be?

Why are we not prepared to spend our lives—from birth to death —just living? And what do we mean by that?

Things happen to us. Some things make us happy; other things make us unhappy. We would rather be happy than unhappy, and so we pursue those things that we believe will make us happy and try to avoid those things that we believe will make us unhappy. It is all very logical—and obviously sense! Only a fool would pursue those things that he believes will make him unhappy!

But what is "happy"?

Happiness is . . . a warm fire. But not in the middle of a summer heatwave.

Happiness is . . . a friend you love. But not when you are rejected.

Happiness is . . . a job well done. But *then* what?

Happiness is . . . getting to your destination. But *then* what?

What is "happy"?

Is happiness something that we one day hope to have?

No, of course it isn't. We have all been *happy*—how else can we discuss the subject at all? If we have never been happy, then happiness as a word can have no meaning for us.

And, what is more, there are times when we know we are happy. What is it that we then know? Why are we happy? What happens to the "happiness"? Where does it "go"? And, having "gone", how can we get it back again?

I want to be happy; don't you?

But do I know what I mean by that; do you?

If I, now, set out on a long journey—and my destination is a land where I am told that I will be "happy", what is more important, the journey that I am about to make to this land, or my arrival there?

Think about it: We are setting out on a journey; we have an aim; we know where we are going; is not the journey of supreme importance?

In the age that we live in there have been many experiments made by innumerable people to arrive in the land of happiness *without making the journey*. People have taken drugs, have indulged sexually, have imbibed alcohol . . . what happens after the drugs wear off, after the sexual experience has drained us, after the alcohol has passed through the body? We are back where we started . . . wanting happiness again. It seems that none of the external agents that Man resorts to can transport him to happiness and allow him *consciously to remain there*.

Perhaps for this reason, more than any other, the religious teachers over the centuries came to be listened to. They offered a way for each of us to try to fulfil the "heart's desire".

Consider: You and I were once, in historical time, babies beginning our confrontation with life on earth.

When I was a baby did I want to be "happy"?

Did I consciously *want* anything?

I simply *was*; and, in *being*, I was at the beginning of a journey. That journey is the Buddha Way.

*

In Buddhist terms, the baby is in *samsara*.

As with many concepts and terms in the tradition of Buddhism, *samsara* as a word carries different meanings according to the degree of understanding of experience, but in this context we may take it to mean a state in which "spirit" has come into being in the world, has begun a phase of physical existence, has entered the birth-death cycle.

I have been born and I will die.

This in no way explains who I am, where I came from, why I am here, nor where I will go to; however, the plain facts are: I was born, I will die.

If we look at a baby—a baby such as you and I once were—we are looking at a potential person. We might say that he or she is innocent—in the sense that the being is as yet virtually unimpressed by the world and can do no harm. Little has happened to it, except it has been born. (Little! That "birth" is itself beyond our comprehension! We cannot repeat often enough: Where did the life come from? What is it? Why is it here?)

What do we mean by "innocence"?

Look at a baby—a baby such as you and I once were—does it "believe" anything? Is it capable of wilfully hurting or offending? Is it capable of wilfully pleasing? Is it capable of being consciously selfish?

Innocence. You and I were innocent . . .

A human being ... being human ... potentially capable of becoming a mature, adult member of the species Man.

What is the purpose of that potential?

How may that potential purpose be fulfilled?

Look at a baby—like a sheet of paper waiting for the writing.

You and I were once like that ... innocent.

*

Is it simply that as creatures you and I may partake in the procreation and survival of the species?

Or is the purpose to compete with other humans to acquire wealth and fame, to achieve a position of power and influence over others? Such a life may help to enhance the status and privilege of one society over another, and may be laudable in the eyes of that society; but has it anything to do with man's purpose?

Or is the aim to direct human endeavour to outwit nature and by scientific knowledge and technology secure the survival of an ever-increasing human population on earth?

Or is the aim to enjoy as much pleasure as can be contrived in the span of a life, whether or not at the expense of other human beings?

Are any of these ends in themselves?

Can we find in such alternatives the reason for man's being here on earth—for my being here, for your being here; for man's evolution over thousands of years? The Buddhist answer would be an emphatic "No!" Towards what goal have we advanced?

May we find in any or all of these the highest purpose of human potential—and that means *my* potential and *your* potential. *I* am the result of thousands and thousands of years of evolution. *I* am the potential next step for mankind. And the same is true for you. All of us, here now, are the result of Man's past; all of us, here now, are the potential for Man's future. It is quite a daunting thought.

When each of us asks "Why am I here?" and "Why was I born?" the questions are not just for ourselves, but for humanity.

And if I seek to be "happy"—being as I am the potential next step for Man ... the happiness is not for me alone; is it?

*

Let us live happily without hating those who hate us. Let us be free from hatred among those who hate.

Let us live happily; among the ailing let us live in health.

Let us live happily, free from greed among the greedy.

Let us live happily, though we call nothing our own. Let us be like the gods, feeding on love.

Victory breeds hatred, for the conquered is unhappy. The calm one is he who has given up both victory and defeat ...

... He who goes with fools has a long journey; company with fools is as painful as being with an enemy; company with the wise is as pleasant as meeting with friends.

Therefore one should follow the wise, the intelligent and the noble; one should follow them like the moon in the path of the stars.

(The DHAMMAPADA)

*

And of course such sentiments are not exclusively Buddhist; they belong to all the faith-inspired religions—what, in this series of books, we have called the faith religions.

Religion is man-invented.

The human mind has the extraordinary capacity of being able to consider the phenomenon of existence. In other words, man becomes conscious of himself. This capacity provokes profound questions in the mind about the nature of existence, its purpose and fulfilment. And, broadly speaking, Man's attempts to answer such questions gives rise to religion.

Religions, in one form or another, propose causes, means and goals in relation to resolving those questions.

We discussed the growth of religion—and particularly the religion that has become known as Buddhism in the last chapter—but it may be worth pausing for a moment here to consider a strange aspect of all religions.

Each one of them sprang from the experiences and observations of an individual or group of individuals as they passed through the samsaric world; the cycle of birth and death.

You and I—all of us—are in the samsaric world now. Our experience and our observation of that experience is no different in essence from the experiences and observations of Gautama, or Jesus, Moses or Mohammed . . . the potential is in each of us.

And, what is more, when such men first related their observations and expressed their inspiration they were not doing so in a formal religious context. In every aspect it was only *later* that the religion was formed, not by them but by their disciples.

And later still those originators became objects of worship for their followers and were invested by them with the special attributes that set them apart from ordinary men to the point of being almost "gods".

But if they were gods, then they were also subject to birth and death and all the experiences of the samsaric world. For what is essential in each of the teachings is that the founder—the Gautama, the Jesus, or whoever—was, it is claimed in each case, a *man*, living, breathing, eating and drinking, sleeping and waking; like you and like me.

If they have the qualities that deserve worship from their followers—then, at least potentially, may not you and may not I also have those qualities?

One of the difficulties of religion for a person who is not yet committed to that religion is that it seems to be based on experiences that are not common to all men. In other words the religious founders were apparently super-men, special in every way—and indeed many religions would deem it a blasphemy for a disciple to say "I am the same as him." Or even, "I am Divine."

And, of course, we have only to look at the chaos and the strife in the world as we know it, so much of which stems directly or indirectly from man's greed, his lust, his ignorance and his selfish strivings, to see that Man is far from being what we think of as "God" or what we think of as "good".

But let us return to our new-born baby; to *any* new-born baby, *any at all*.

Is the baby greedy, selfish, ignorant, lustful? We would not even consider such terms for the innocent being that we look at.

*

What fate awaits that baby?

Discounting for the purposes of this book all the mundane possibilities for achievements or failures in the world's terms, and concentrating on the religious aspirations only, in what way may religion—the formulated experiences of the religious founders—help or hinder this baby to develop the potential that is its essential nature?

At this point the baby is not a Buddhist, nor a Christian, nor a Hindu, nor a Muslim, nor a Jew (in the religious sense).

No one is born *belonging* to a religion.

The family or society in which each of us grew up may well have introduced us to a particular religion through a form of initiation. As each of us developed, so our minds may have been indoctrinated with that religion's teachings and practices, just as we were indoctrinated with political attitudes, moral concepts, social codes and an economic tradition.

But is any baby *born* a "Buddhist" or whatever?

Is any baby *born* a "Communist" or whatever?

Is any baby *born* morally "sound", socially "acceptable", economically "solvent"?

The nature of the potential in the child may dictate that he or she will, in due course, become religious, but the introduction to a particular form of religion will not necessarily guarantee that that religiousness will manifest and bear fruit.

And is this not equally true about all other attitudes, concepts, codes and structures with which we are indoctrinated during those first, early years in the samsaric world?

24

They simply give a particular context through which we may evolve. (And there is evidence—in the authors' own experience for example—that strong indoctrination particularly in the religious context, can stunt the natural development of religiousness. Unintelligent preaching and repetition of dogma may well have the opposite effect to that naively intended; it may result in indiscriminate submission or frustrated rejection. Or it may, most significantly, start us questioning for *ourselves*—and therefore not necessarily "in line" with the original preaching and dogma.)

So what manner of context would the Buddhist tradition give to a child?

In the following chapters we will consider some of the concepts attributed to the historical figure Gautama and the subsequent Buddhist tradition—but we must again emphasize that these, of necessity, will be the authors' interpretations, for there is no such thing as an absolute and incontrovertible definition of such concepts. There never was, there never can be. A thing is only what it does to you or to me; a thing only means what it does to you or to me. You cannot have faith for me, believe for me, see for me; neither can I for you.

The experience and the observation of that experience belongs to the individual alone.

And rather than present these concepts simply as theories that may be believed or not, we hope to convey that, at least during the preliminary stages of "the Way", the propositions are easily observable in our own experience, whether we be labelled "Buddhist" or not.

*

By oneself evil is done; by oneself one suffers. By oneself evil is left undone, by oneself one is purified. Purity and impurity are personal concerns. No one can purify another.

Let no man neglect his own duty for another's. Clearly seeing what is best for him, let a man attend to it.

(The DHAMMAPADA)

*

But we do need help.

You may not be able to see for me—but you can point out where I should be looking in order that I may see what you think is important for me.

You may play the harp skilfully, but you require that I should skilfully listen.

You may have a wonderful gift, but it is nothing if there is no one to give it to.

Gautama offered as a gift his experiences and the observation of those experiences in order that we might see for ourselves.

*

It is generally accepted that Gautama was born about two thousand five hundred years ago in a village called Kapilavatha, in the state now called Bihar in eastern India. His family was wealthy, powerful and aristocratic and he was brought up in a secure and privileged section of society. It is said that until he was about thirty years old his life was so secluded and protected that he had no knowledge of the world outside the palace in which he lived. In fact it seems that he was deliberately shielded from any experience that might upset his happiness—anything ugly, cruel, threatening, fearful, distasteful—anything that might cause him to be worried or frightened.

Whether this be fact or fiction, it is poignant to consider how this contrasts with our own experience. And certainly we can imagine how such an unusual introduction to life would have pre-conditioned his mind to such a biased view that the drama of the events which followed would have been heightened to a degree that we cannot possibly appreciate. Imagine living right through to mature adulthood without ever having been discomforted by any threat whatsoever to one's equanimity and happiness!

The story continues that when he was about thirty Gautama set his heart on going for a journey outside the palace. Hearing of this plan, his father arranged a pleasure excursion for his beloved son. But first he gave orders that all people with any kind of affliction should be kept away from the royal route. Very gently all the cripples, all the crazy, the aged and the ailing, all the beggars and the poor, were removed from the sides of the road.

But the best laid plans go astray and, on his journey, Gautama encountered an *old man*, and later a *man with a diseased body*, and later still *a corpse*.

The shock was traumatic for Gautama. He was experiencing the outside world, and the outside world filled him with horror.

After the shock came pain and sorrow and profound concern to understand.

Thus, as a result of these experiences, Siddhartha Gautama began his search for Truth and the theme on which he concentrated was the nature of suffering.

Why should there be suffering?

Having come into the world, why should there be pain and sorrow, decay and death?

Is there, he demanded, any escape?

*

When we look at the baby, we may wish for it a healthy and happy life—and, in doing so, we would not be unlike Gautama's father—but we know that inevitably it will have its share of pain and sorrow also.

Why?

What is the point of the unhappiness that it will undoubtedly experience—the various forms of "ill-state" which the Buddhists call *dukkha*?

Can it be due to some imperfections in the baby's constitution?

If so, where do the imperfections come from?

Is it the baby's fault if it sets out in life with imperfections?

Now you were once a baby and I was once a baby and we are considering another baby.

No two babies are alike; in other words, each human being, right from birth, is unique. That is obvious from the point of view of physical appearance. But it would seem that it is also true of the inherent character, disposition, nature—whatever we care to call it.

Because, again obviously, no two babies can be born from the same mother *simultaneously* (not even twins emerge at precisely the same moment, and even the strange phenomenon of "Siamese twins", though linked, still emerge one at a time) and can never be in exactly the same place at the same time, and because it would be impossible to simulate exactly the same environment and experience for two babies over a long enough period, it is not at all clear what elements in behaviour are attributable to the original character and what elements are the result of that character's reaction to, and moulding by, the influences of environment.

For example, what is anger? Is it a self-originating disposition, regardless of outside influence, or is it only derived from interaction with the environment?

It is very difficult to disentangle causes in the area of human behaviour but it is generally accepted that each human being is born with an individual and original pattern of characteristics.

In other words, the differences between people cannot be totally accounted for by the differences in their circumstances and experience.

Gautama may have had the experience of his peculiarly protected upbringing. But when he experienced the world it was his own particular nature which made him react in the manner described above. He could have easily wanted to get back into the palace and never go out again.

What would have been the normal and perfect reaction to his experience?

Although there may be some vaguely assessable average or balanced constitution (based usually upon the common experience of the greatest number of people), no one can define what is normal or perfect.

Who ever heard of a baby having a "perfect" character?

By what criteria could a baby be judged "normal" or "perfect"?

Usually a baby is claimed to be perfect—by the parents at least—if it does not appear to have any physical defect (and, as far as the

28

parents are concerned, it is "beautiful", whatever it looks like to anyone else) and it is "normal" if, as far as those who are looking after it are concerned, it is "no trouble".

But how consistently and for how long is a baby "perfect"?

Is it perfect only in the estimation of others or can it be perfect in itself—or to itself?

Or, to put it another way, can a baby be "imperfect"?

How can it be? It simply is itself, a unique baby. How can anything unique be "imperfect"?

*

So we have suffering and we have a striving for perfection.

Could suffering be useful in that *through* it we might understand something?

Could the understanding of perfection be the purpose of life?

Could birth into the life-death cycle, *samsara*, offer one simple opportunity—to realize the mystery of itself, of *life*?

Is the experience, any experience, the all important key?

*

Watchfulness is the path to immortality, and thoughtlessness the path to death.

The watchful do not die, but the thoughtless are already like the dead.

(The DHAMMAPADA)

*

Plainly the nature and disposition of the baby—no matter how perfect or imperfect in relation to an as yet unknown absolute standard of excellence—gives it a kind of basic and individual platform from which to begin to experience the world and respond to it.

And its reaction to that experience—how it copes with it and is influenced by it—will reinforce or modify the original and individual character.

So where does the individual character come from?

29

One explanation may be genetics—that it is in some way inherited through a permutation of gene "information", part derived from the father and part from the mother. But is that not another of our diverting and superficial factual "answers"? The observation and description of a microscopic bio-chemical process may demonstrate the physical means of transmission, but does it help me to understand the living mystery of my own character as I experience it? How does the scientific information concerning my genes relate to my experience of being me? How do I experience being part of my father or part of my mother?

How did I become the person I am?

Am I the product of part-father-part-mother interacting over a number of years with the accident of circumstance?

If I am "imperfect", in what way am I imperfect and whose fault is it?

And can I do anything about my "imperfection"?

*

> ... To set up what you like against what you dislike—
> That is the disease of the mind:
> When the deep meaning of the Way is not understood,
> Peace of mind is disturbed to no purpose.
>
> The Way is perfect like unto vast space,
> With nothing wanting, nothing superfluous.
> It is indeed due to making choice
> That its Suchness is lost sight of ...

> (SENG-TS'AN, On Believing in Mind)

*

The Buddhist tradition speaks of karma.

This is a very complex and subtle concept and it requires continual consideration and re-appraisal as new aspects and realizations about human nature—especially our own natures—evolve through years of experience and attempting to understand.

Thus, if we say that the individual's basic or essential nature is the result of, and is dictated by, "former lives", then there are numerous traps and assumptions that we may fall into.

"Former lives" in terms of logical, passing time and sequential thinking suggests a succession of consecutive re-births, of reincarnation through time, but we should be very wary of drawing mental models and jumping to conclusions from such a limited method of thinking. It would be wise for us in this context, and in many others in the religious and philosophical realm, not to become committed to definite conclusions and ways of thinking about something. Let us form a mental model and try it, by all means, and if it helps for the moment, well and good; but always let us be prepared to revise it in the light of further experience and understanding. This may sound obvious and reasonable—but it is amazing how many people think they have found complete answers and become resistant to the possibility of having to revise their belief, especially when they have become established and noted for their success and conviction.

*

"Former lives" ... the idea is rich with possibilities for the explanation of mysteries.

But ... whose former life?

Who or what can be said to re-incarnate?

Who travels round "the wheel of birth-death, birth-death"?

How does it start and how does it end?

How can we comprehend eternity in which there is no such thing as the beginning or ending of anything?

What may perfect itself in this process and how?

These are vast questions.

The most enticing trap in the idea of *karma* is that I should adopt it as a reasonable model through which I can conceive of *my* continuation—that I transmigrate from one life to the next in succession—and that therefore I need not worry about the next death.

But who or what is the "I" who transmigrates?

What carries over from one life to the next?

Before we can home in on a deepening penetration of the concept, it is crucial always to refer to the question that dominates this book, and of the others in this series.

"*Who am I?*"

Unless the mind becomes clearer and clearer as to who I am or am not, what real validity can there be in the belief that I am re-born from life to life?

*

Now the reader by this time may have become hopelessly confused, because we, the authors, have just taken a huge leap into one of the basic doctrines of the Buddha teaching—*karma*. We have done so without any fore-warning, without any preparation.

But this has not been an entirely wilful or accidental shift of direction on our part. For it seems that this is how such concepts are approached. They emerge from seemingly "nowhere", and are first encountered as "meaningless". Once encountered, the concept belongs to me—or to you—and may be considered throughout all of "time" whenever we are mindful and always supposing that the concept interests us.

The new-born baby is not prepared for any thing; it simply awaits the confrontation.

Thus metal is not prepared for rust—it simply encounters rust at a given "time". Where does rust come from?

In encountering the concept of *karma* in this way, we are, in effect experiencing karmic law in action.

> *The iron itself createth the rust,*
> *Which slowly is bound to consume it.*
> *The evil-doer by his own deeds*
> *Is led to a life full of suffering.*

(The DHAMMAPADA)

*

So, here we are, encountering for the first time the Buddhist law of *karma*.

(And we will need a deep understanding of this law if we are to cope with the Buddhist notion that, according to the doctrine of the *karma*, "I" may in the next life be incarnated in the form of a dog or a snake or a whatever. If I think that it is *me* that is reborn, then the possibility of becoming a dog or a snake is either a horrific fate or superstitious rubbish . . . and perhaps a part of the doctrine that I would prefer to ignore!)

But let us take *karma* a little further.

In one sense it can be thought of as the fateful blueprint with which each of us begins his or her life. If I think of it as *my karma*, then it is reasonable to suppose that one purpose of my life will be to take advantage of its good aspects, and to resist, ameliorate or resolve the effects of its "bad" aspects. This modifies the scope of *karma* for it suggests that it is not some crystallized and permanent disposition which I have to live with all my life—but that it is a continuing, ever-present "filter" for my behaviour which can be modified, for better or worse, in terms of increasing or decreasing happiness or contentment. And further, that there may be a responsibility here—that it is not just a case of increasing my happiness or improving my success but that in modifying the negative aspects I improve the "atmosphere" for those around me and for those who come after me.

In other words, being given a gift, we must give back in return.

The skilful playing of a harp is a gift—but if the skilful listener has gone, then we cut the strings as a mark of true friendship; for the gift that we were given was a gift for the listener and never for us to keep to ourselves.

*

It is not easy to summarize all the implications of *karma*.

For example, linked with the above aspect, is the proposition that *karma* operates as a law. This law is inherent in the motive of any action . . . that the nature of the cause or motive will have direct reciprocation in the nature of the effect or result of that action. So, to the extent that my actions are influenced by my distrust of others so the effects of those actions will seem to endorse the idea that others distrust me.

This aspect of *karma* is very subtle and is primarily to do with mind ... how beliefs about ourselves are created and established and the limitations such beliefs put on our ability to think, speak and act naturally and appropriately. It is very much the realm of "how you judge, so will you be judged;" the more generous you are, the more generous life will be to you; the more you love, the more you will be loved; and so on.

Very often this concept is taken on the crude level of cause and effect in the physical realm. For example, that if you murder someone, then someone will murder you. This would be difficult to substantiate and, in terms of a single life, would appear to be untrue.

But let us leave aside consideration of *karma* at this level and consider it simply in terms of our own mental experience in this life.

At this level it seems a fair proposition and it is one in which we may more easily understand several aspects of Buddhist teaching in relation to how we should think, speak and behave *here* and *now*.

It would seem to be a very reasonable proposition that as I behave so others will behave towards me. The more I am able to love, the more likely I am to be loved; the more I hate, the more I will be hated. The more selfish and violent my motive and effort to obtain what I think I want, the less likely I am to receive what I really need.

In other words, the more harm I do, the more diseased and wounded will my own psyche become.

Never is an action called "well done", which makes us suffer afterwards,
Of which we reap the fruit in tears, with weeping, wailing and lament.

34

That action only is "well done", which brings no suffering in its train,
Of which we reap the fruit quite glad, in happiness, with joyous heart.

(The DHAMMAPADA)

*

So, *karma* is a difficult concept but, as we look at the innocent new-born baby we begin to see a possibility.

The baby was born unique—which means, in the context of *karma*, that the spirit or life entering that body has come into a particular karmic existence.

I am in the karmic existence of this body.

The "I" in that baby's body and the "I" in this body is the same.

The difference is that the "I" in me sees the universe through the karmic dispensation of my body, giving rise to the experience of being "me", whilst the "I" in the baby's body sees the universe through the karmic dispensation of that body, which gives rise to the baby's experience of being him or her.

No, it is not easy to comprehend!

The "I" in me and the "I" in you is the same enlivening spirit or life.

And that "I" has a common purpose—to master and perfect the *karma* in me and the *karma* in you.

You were once a new-born baby.

I was once a new-born baby.

Look at a photograph of yourself as a baby. Can you believe it? Can you in any way associate the "you" who is here now, with the "you" who was there then?

It is almost like a "former life", isn't it?

But the "I" was there then, the "I" is here now.

Who am I?

Three

Bassui wrote the following letter to one of his disciples who was about to die:

"The essence of your mind is not born, so it will never die. It is not an existence, which is perishable. It is not an emptiness, which is a mere void. It has neither colour nor form. It enjoys no pleasures and suffers no pains.

"I know you are very ill. Like a good Zen student, you are facing that sickness squarely. You may not know exactly who is suffering, but question yourself: What is the essence of this mind? Think only of this. You will need no more. Covet nothing. Your end which is endless is as a snowflake dissolving in the pure air.

Zen story

*

"Your end which is endless . . ."

How did the snowflake begin? Where did it come from?

How does the snowflake end? Where does it go to?

The logical mind, conditioned to think in terms of passing time, sequence and continuity, tends to assume a given situation as being preceded by an ordered succession of events traceable back into an ever-receding past and being succeeded by a projected continuing of that order into an indefinite future.

Mind—logical mind—therefore tends to believe in beginnings, continuings and endings, all taking place *in the world's time*.

But this way of thinking presents certain problems:

Can I ever trace back to the original "beginning"; the "beginning", say, of the first snowflake?

How did it happen?

36

Was it sudden and spontaneous?

How was it brought about ... if not by "something" which preceded it?

A beginning, *in historical time*, always presents the mind with an insurmountable block—because it will always want to reach back *before* any beginning that it can conceive of.

The nursury conundrum "Which came first, the chicken or the egg?" is no trite amusement for infant minds when viewed in this light! You need an egg to hatch a chicken, you need a chicken to hatch an egg ... The mind is awed by the simplicity with which its limitations are exposed, shrugs off the riddle as childish nonsense and either ignores the question, claiming it to be "unimportant", or seeks back through the evolutionary chain of what we have called fact-answers, and thereby avoids it. What, however, remains apparent is that the mind cannot answer the question.

Which came first, the chicken or the egg?

And so also with endings.

Will you know when you are dead?

How can we conceive of a final ending?

What would it be like?

Would it be some kind of sudden, total annihilation?

Would the final, ultimate ending be a complete self-destruction of the universe ... into what? An inconceivable "nothing"?

And how would this come about? At the instigation of some agency? Then, presumably the agency would itself still exist and continue?

A final ending also then presents the mind with an insurmountable block ... because, although it may have to admit the possible ending of itself at death, it will always want to reach beyond any possible ending it can conceive of. It assumes that the universe will continue after its death.

Once I am committed to the belief in continuing time in which all processes take place, I am committed to beginnings and endings in time, and cannot cope with such a concept as the beginning and ending *of time itself.*

37

This conditioning of mind that is experienced by the *being* in the the samsaric world is entirely based upon the *finite*.

What happens, then, when the in-finite concepts present themselves to mind?

Let us consider a simple example—and one particularly relevant to the age in which we live (or, more precisely, through which we are *apparently* "passing").

We have, in the last twenty years experienced the first tentative steps in physical space travel. Men have walked on the moon; man-made machines have travelled to Mars and beyond ... It is a stimulating prospect. But what, so far, has happened? With each progressive "step" outside the earth's atmosphere, a little more of "space" has become finite to mind. The moon has become, as it were, a comprehensible territory of mind. But what lies beyond the moon? The stars. What lies beyond the stars? More stars. And beyond that? More stars. What lies beyond the outer regions of space? More space. What lies beyond farthest space? Still more space. Where does space *end*? And, if there is an end ... what lies beyond that?

The mind can become physically exhausted and disturbed trying to comprehend the infinite.

And yet the infinite questions present themselves to mind!

From somewhere, somehow, questions arise that we simply are not equipped—through logical mind—to answer.

Can this really be so?

Or are we always, through mind, "looking in the wrong direction"?

What is it that we want to know—and why do we want to know it?

Between birth and death, within the finite, the samsaric world—there is a "living". Why then should we be plagued by such infinite, disturbing and unanswerable questions as "What lies beyond space?"

*

As a fletcher straightens his arrow, so the wise man straightens his unsteady mind, which is so hard to control.

The mind struggles to escape the tempter, as a fish thrown on dry land.

It is good to train the wandering mind. A mind under control brings great happiness ...

Knowing that the body is as fragile as a jar, and making the mind as firm as a fortress, one should attack the tempter with the weapon of wisdom, and guard one's conquest carefully.

Before long the body will lie on the ground, cast aside and devoid of consciousness, like a useless log of wood.

Whatever a hater may do to one he hates, or an enemy to his enemy, a wrongly directed mind will do greater evil.

Neither father nor mother nor any other relative will do a man so much good as a well directed mind ...

(The DHAMMAPADA)

*

As man grapples, in this mode of thinking, with mysteries for which his explanations and speculations are never provable by logical thinking, he is forced into having "faith" in concepts whose validity he cannot prove. In turn this presents him with further considerable difficulties—for how can he be sure that "faith" is not just another word for self-persuasion or make-believe?

We could say that it is through this process that the phenomenon "religion" emerges ... in the sense that the fundamental concepts on which religion is based cannot be proved as valid by human "thinking".

However, the piece from the Dhammapada, quoted above, suggests that The Buddha Way is to control the very act of *thinking* —the activity in mind itself.

This is a very significant point in our consideration of the Buddha's teaching as compared with the other religious teachings that we have been looking at in this series.

Whereas many religions—Christianity, Judaism, Islam, and to

a certain extent the Vedanta of Hinduism—present the aspirant with the concept of a *deity*, a super-human, all-knowing, omniscient *being* (albeit invisible, and, most essentially, outside the samsaric cycle of birth and death), a *god* who knows what we do not know, nor shall ever know in this life, Buddha presents no such idea to us.

Buddha, let us remind ourselves again, means "enlightened one". The "enlightened one" was a man—fleshed, breathing, *living in this world*.

This is in no way disputing nor denying the efficacy of the god-image. Far from it. If the god-image enables a person to transcend the limitations of ordinary mind, then the god-image is the essential agent on that person's way to "enlightenment".

There is a tendency with a god-image to stop working for ourselves; to "leave it all to God". If by that a person means "surrender", then that person is blessed indeed; if however, it means lazy indulgence in the habitual round of involvement in the cycle of sense gratification and sense desire, then the god-image ceases to be more than a sop to our "conscience" and does not really work in us at all. If that is the case—then what really is the difference between the person who says he "believes in god" and the atheist who wants nothing to do with such a concept?

"Enlighten" is defined in the dictionary as: "*Instruct, inform, (person on subject); shed light on (object); give light to (person); free (person) from prejudice or superstition.*"

That would seem to us a fair description of what we mean by "religion". That is the platform from which we are working. And, as such, *any thing* that "enlightens" us is valid and vital to our consideration of the Question of Religion.

*

> *... Pursue not the outer entanglements,*
> *Dwell not in the inner Void;*
> *Be serene in the oneness of things,*
> *And dualism vanishes by itself.*

When you strive to gain quiescence by stopping motion,
The quiescence thus gained is ever in motion;
As long as you tarry in the dualism,
How can you realize oneness?

And when oneness is not thoroughly understood,
In two ways loss is sustained:
The denying of reality is the asserting of it,
And the asserting of emptiness is the denying of it . . .

(SENG-TS'AN, *On Believing in Mind*)

*

Our hypothetical baby begins his or her venture in the "ocean" of *samsara*, innocent.

As such it has no concept of duality.

For the baby at this stage there is simply existence. In whatever way we may conceive of "spirit" or "life" we may say that it has entered a new, physical form which has resulted in the baby's experience of being human . . . the "is-ness" or "being" as experienced in the human form.

It is as simple as that for the baby.

The baby simply *is*.

And we may surmise that one of the most significant features of this state, as opposed to what will happen later, is that the baby does not *think* itself as *being separate* from the world around it.

It has no mental concept of itself nor of the world; so not only does it not think of itself as separate from the world but it does not even have knowledge of it either.

If it were able to conceive of anything in its mind, if it were able to formulate any thought as to its situation, it might simply say, "I AM"—as a description or simple statement of its having come into being.

As a drop of dew merges into the ocean, so a baby enters "life", or *vice versa*.

The dew is both a drop and the ocean—they co-exist as one; the baby is both a being in human form and a part of "life"—they co-exist as one.

Which came first, the ocean or the dew, "life" or the being?

*

For, of course, inevitably there is a development from that innocent state.

Reluctant though it may be (not consciously so but "instinctively") the baby has no option but to grow physically and to develop mental processes—providing it is not "abnormal" (and how can anything unique be "abnormal"?).

The world would have it that "abnormality" in a child, especially mental abnormality, is an unfortunate "accident", an imperfection due to genetic flaw, difficult birth, or whatever. But supposing—for example in the case of child autism—we think of it in another way. Perhaps the "spirit" of the child is reluctant to lose its innocence and undertake the challenge inherent in the process of development? Maybe it "knows" or "remembers" the consequences of participating in the ways of the world? Why should we assume that the baby does not have an innate and fully developed will and intelligence at birth? Could it not be that it has, but does not at that stage have a body or mind developed enough to be able to express and communicate them in a way which we can understand?

Speculation, certainly—but leading to an interesting thought, for, if this were to be the case, then the baby is both innocent *and* possessing of will and intelligence. Two things would arise out of this: Firstly that the loss of innocence is not dependent upon *gaining* of will and intelligence, and secondly that having will and being intelligent would not necessarily bar us from the "is-ness" of the baby state, now, here, in our *present* state.

We do not consciously remember now the state of innocence of ourselves as babies—because the mental "apparatus" had not been developed to be able to conceive of or realize the nature of existence. But then certain developments took place that we may remember.

Even if we do not, we may easily observe what does happen to any baby.

The child begins to *learn*.

*

This is a many-faceted and complex process but let us make one or two simple suggestions about it because it is central to the theme of Gautama's teaching.

Never *mind* how it is done, but we begin to associate certain verbal sound-forms (words, for example) with certain sensory impressions. At first it will be single sounds or words associated with visual images—"mother", "father", items of food and drink, clothing, and defecation, and so on. Items related to our immediate comfort and survival. Later the vocabulary will extend, as the range of our senses extends, to the less intimate and immediately demanding— "dog", "tree", "sea", "sun", "stars" . . .

The most immediate learning will be in response to and in relation to physical feelings and requirements—the desire for comfort, contentment, security, in the form of food, drink and loving touch. And, complementary to that, the rejection of or reaction to that which appears to be causing discomfort, discontent, insecurity.

We begin to respond positively or negatively according to feelings and sensations stimulated and aroused within ourselves. As we learn to identify the sources of the desirable and the undesirable, we begin to store them in memory.

Herein lies the root of a dichotomy which in a more elaborate and sophisticated manner will persist right through our lives— unless, later, we realize the consequences of it and endeavour to overcome it.

Like and dislike.

Attraction and repulsion.

Desire and aversion.

This is a dualism that we begin to learn very early in our lives.

And it is natural and right that we should do so—for several practical reasons.

I could not begin to undertake my role in life if I did not learn from experience how and where to acquire that which will ensure my physical survival and how to avoid that which will harm or threaten the chances of that survival.

You don't put your hand in the flame twice! Not intentionally. For the flame will burn you and the burning will not only hurt but it will, if allowed, destroy you. The aversion—to the pain—is therefore useful to the survival.

But then we come to more subtle developments and questions.

To what extent are *all* our fears and desires valid?

May there not be some which are out of proportion, exaggerated, too dominant?

*

For physical survival what do I *need*?

Basically, certain intake and certain conditions. I need adequate air, food, liquid, clothing and shelter. That's all.

How then does it come about that if I manage to acquire my daily needs in these respects that the need spills over into excess?

Why is it that *greed* ever occurs?

And what about all the other pleasures that I pursue, even although I do not actually need them?

Why do any of us want more than that which is actually necessary for our survival?

Beyond the fundamental and universal desires and fears which enable each of us to exist, do we not also come to acquire a catalogue of likes and dislikes which apparently have nothing to do with essential need?

Such questions are, of course, vast in their ramifications and we can hardly begin to explore them here, but the point is that all manner of desire and fear begins to emerge in a child as a result of its learning about the world and its own particular dispensation in comparison with others.

For, in learning about the world and in becoming conscious of

44

itself in relation to others, a child learns to think of itself as *separate* from the world—and that means all other people in the world as well.

We each of us learn to think of ourselves as separate, particular, distinct and even peculiar!

As a new being we were seen to be unique in terms of creation; now we begin to believe in ourselves as unique in terms of the world.

Is a drop of dew unique? Or is it only unique in its particular and even peculiar, exclusive creation?

As such, the drop of dew "is"; that is all. It is one with all the other drops of dew in the ocean; it is one with the ocean; it is the ocean.

Is a baby unique? Or is it only unique in its particular and even peculiar, exclusive creation?

As such, the baby "is"; that is all. It is one with all babies; it is one with life; it is life.

But then we begin to believe in our separate existence, and, because we see that everyone else is concerned to survive, we learn competition. Put in simple terms, we come to believe that our survival will be ensured if, in relation to others, we acquire more ... strength, agility, power, influence, ability, learning, wealth, fame, and so on. (And by survival in the broadest sense, we also mean the security of status and recognized identity. If, for example, I come top in an exam or win a race, then I am more likely to be noted by others and my reputation will be enhanced.)

This does not mean that we necessarily enter competition ruthlessly or aggressively, or at the expense of others (although two people cannot win a race—or if they do, then the "glory" must be shared). Whether we do this as children or later in life will depend on character and the availability of resources and hence whether actual survival is threatened or not. None of us can actually say whether we would kill another human being for food, say, until we are put in the situation of having to do so in order to survive—and at that time a great deal will depend upon how much we value our own life. Nevertheless, in a stable society with adequate resources for all, these are the conditions we tend to find and these are our basic motives; *we compete*, even though in a sophisticated and civilized society our competitiveness may be graced by such labels as "human endeavour", "human progress", "cultural development", "social service", "scientific advance" and so on. Why should any of us do anything—without some motive to spur us on?

This is, of course, looking at development from the viewpoint of physical survival. It is easy to forget in a developed, industrialized nation, where to a great extent it is not threatened, that such survival lies as the basic motive of education. Beneath the veneer of political and economic ideologies it lies dormant when affairs are more or less stable; but should these ideologies begin to fail when wealth and resources are depleted then it shows through quickly enough. It is a diametrically opposed viewpoint and motive to one that we may later develop—that being the aesthetic, moral, religious or spiritual discipline. This later development is to do with man's "higher" purpose, one which distinguishes him from the animal kingdom which appears to be motivated only by survival.

Our most profound difficulties will be in attempting to reconcile these two differing viewpoints, should they come into confrontation.

Or, if they prove ultimately to be irreconcilable, to settle for one at the expense of the other.

At such a time we may be faced by crucial questions which no one else will be able to answer for us:

"To what am I prepared to devote my life?"

"What am I prepared to die for?"

*

He whose appetites are controlled, who cares little about food, who realizes the unreality of all things, his path is like that of the birds in the air.

Even the gods must envy him whose senses are under control like well-trained horses, and who has put away pride and evil thoughts.

46

He who is tolerant like the earth, firm as a pillar, and as clear as a mountain pool, such a man will never be reborn.

His mind is peaceful, and his words and deeds. Thus calm is he who has attained deliverance.

(The DHAMMAPADA)

*

And so, in an apparently haphazard fashion, we learn—to like and dislike, to choose, to prefer.

And sooner or later we will become aware of competition. No matter how protected we may have been during our childhood, when we set out on adult life in the world, it will be there, waiting for us.

And with these developments comes trouble!

Not being able to have or to do just what we would like; having to have or to do that which we dislike; the challenge of competition promoting the desire for success and the fear of failure.

And so we begin *to suffer*.

We may think that it would be perfect if we could have and do all the things that we like and be relieved of all the things that we dislike. But advocates and dreamers of that kind of Utopia perhaps not only entertain the impossible but also fail to consider a crucial question:

"Does man suffer for a purpose?"

Or to modify the question rather more subtly:

"Is it that man may understand his purpose through having to suffer?"

Just think about it:

Human nature being what it is, would any of us make any effort at all if we did not suffer?

This is not necessarily to advocate effort for its own sake. It implies a special effort—the effort required to become enlightened.

Nor are we suggesting that suffering is a "necessary evil"; only that it is the "spur" and, above all, that we have the capacity to overcome it.

47

Through intensive exploration of the causes of suffering, Gautama was able to realize the overcoming of it as being the key to man's purpose and salvation.

*

"... I know you are very ill. Like a good Zen student you are facing that sickness squarely. You may not know exactly who is suffering; but question yourself: What is the essence of this mind? Think only of this. You will need no more. Covet nothing. Your end which is endless is as a snowflake dissolving in the pure air."

*

And yet we do suffer.

At first life often does seem unfair. As innocent babies we could all be said to have been born equal. But, as we begin to learn, it is evident that we are not all the same.

Through what we have called karmic dispensation, it is soon apparent that we each have different characteristics which may help or hinder us in our competing in the world's terms. And that quite apart from the advantages or disadvantages accorded to us by the "accident" of circumstance—the status, wealth, privilege, etc., of the family and society that we happen to have been born into.

Could it be that the particular dispensation that you are, as it were, "allocated" is the very one through which you will "suffer" and "realize" precisely what you need to suffer in order to realize what you need to realize?

This would put quite a different complexion on what is otherwise deemed, in the world's terms, the "unfair" advantage or disadvantage of birth.

For is it easier for a rich man or for a poor man to reach enlightenment? And that, ultimately, is all that matters in this life.

In this sense we are all equal in a quite precise and awesome way.

Through our karmic dispensation we have each been given precisely what we require for our enlightenment ... in our own terms.

It does not matter whether you are born a prince or a pauper, handsome or ugly, talented or not so talented (all in the world's

48

terms, remember); the point is that inevitably you will suffer in a manner and degree precisely appropriate to what may be realized by you through that suffering.

And again we should emphasize that this sort of proposition should not swing us round to the idea that therefore suffering is to be welcomed and that the greater our suffering the greater the benefit to be gained. This kind of absurd logic has given rise in the past to all manner of self-abuse, self-torment and so on.

As Gautama found, and as we hope to convey later in this book, such self-imposed disciplines can easily be vain and selfish and motivated by a self-aggrandizement which is the very antipathy of the real surrender which is required.

*

It is very easy in comparing oneself with others to bemoan one's fate and to think that if we had the advantages of others then we would not suffer our particular problems.

But, supposing, as a first disciplinary step, we ceased to compare ourselves with anyone else and got on with understanding our own fate and what it is telling us? Supposing we concentrated on observing in what respects our so-called advantages actually help us and our so-called disadvantages actually hinder us . . . in realizing the *real* purpose of our lives?

Would it not be extremely useful to understand the cause and nature of *our own* suffering?

And suppose further that we discovered that our suffering is *our own fault* . . . that it cannot be blamed on others, on accident of birth, or whatever else we think causes it.

Would that not be a revelation?

It would certainly be in the spirit of the Buddha's teaching to suggest that only to the degree that we are able to take responsibility for our own suffering, and are able to cope with it and understand it, so only then will we be able to help others to understand and overcome theirs.

*

49

As the bee collects honey without destroying the beauty and the scent of the flowers, so should the sage go about the town.

The wise man will not look for the faults of others, nor for what they have done or left undone, but will look rather to his own misdeeds.

Like beautiful flowers, full of colour but without scent, are the well-spoken words of the man who does not act accordingly.

Like beautiful flowers, full of colour and full of scent, are the fruitful words of him who acts accordingly.

(The DHAMMAPADA)

*

How often is charitable effort a way in which a person may divert attention from his or her own suffering. And indeed is this not encouraged in the society we live in today? "Instead of dwelling on your own suffering—look to the suffering of others." And, of course, there is some sense in this. For anything is preferable to a morbid attachment to one's own suffering. But that is not what we are talking about here. Not attachment, but looking—really looking—at suffering in a detached way, looking at it for what one can learn from it. And, having learned, then perhaps we would be ready to help others. But without such discipline charitable effort is of doubtful value, for the way in which it is given can be selfish on the part of the giver and may only be of temporary benefit for the sufferer—for it by-passes the essence of helping someone . . . helping them to help themselves through accepting that their suffering is their own responsibility. Just that and nothing else may possibly free them, when they are ready to be freed. This may seem ruthless in contrast to the sentimental idea of charity but we must not be afraid to admit what actually happens as opposed to what we have been conditioned to think happens.

*

So how do we come to suffer—or, in Buddhist terminology, come to suffer *dukkha*, the "ill-state".

After Gautama, at about the age of thirty, had experienced the

50

traumatic shock of seeing, for the first time, poverty, disease, old-age and death, he immediately resolved to discover the cause and meaning of such suffering; and thence of human existence and purpose itself.

From this moment on his *experience* and the *observation of the experience* was to form the essence of what was to become his *teaching*.

And his *teaching* in its turn was to form the basis of what we now know as Buddhist *belief*.

*

What is belief?

How do we come to believe?

Why do we believe?

As we grow older we experience many, many things; far too many for the individual mind to contain and store (as memory). It is our *karma* that selects those things that will be useful to each of us individually in our journey through the samsaric world. The selection having been made, we *learn* those things . . .

Thus, for example, all babies may enjoy musical sounds, but only certain babies will grow up to be "musical"—and perhaps even become musicians; the *karma* dictates the selection of what is to be learnt through the intensity of certain attraction.

(This, in turn, throws quite a different light on our present education system, where all children are expected to get a grounding in all the basic subjects of the school curricular, and may even be punished if they do not do "well" in certain subjects! This could lead to quite extraordinary psychological problems for the child . . . when in fact the child is simply being obedient to its *karma* and is not bothering with those things that will not be useful to it in its karmic development. But remember—useful only for *enlightenment* and not for the "ways of the world".)

Once those things that will be useful have been *learned*, we begin to *believe* in them.

Again let us take a simple example: Having experienced burning a hand in the fire, we learn that fire burns us; and, having learned that fire burns us, we come to believe in the concept of fire as a burning agent.

But our belief does not tell us anything at all about the fire; it does not lead to a knowledge of what "fire" *is*. Indeed, it does quite the reverse, it stands between us and a full understanding of "fire".

"Believe" is defined in the dictionary as: "to regard as true; to accept as true what is said by: to suppose . . . to be firmly persuaded; to have faith (in, on); to judge . . ."

Really penetrating the mental process called "believing" reveals much—for believing is "giving your-Self away". The mind, in committing itself (and therefore "me") to trust in the ephemeral and transitory explanations of this world, *gives itself* to that which is of no lasting value.

In the formative years it may be appropriate that we are led to put our trust in certain knowledge—for our own protection. But we also believe things which, although protective to a degree, can only become fetters which may later bind us and deceive us.

Religious doctrine may be an example of *belief* standing in the way of *Truth*.

Enlightenment is the full blaze of the light of Truth.

Belief in any thing is a substitute for understanding Truth.

In believing, "I lease my being", put my trust in, that which will pass away. No "thing" that I believe in can give me absolute security. By choosing to believe in some thing, I create my own suffering . . . for the thing is not ultimately Truth—and Truth is all that I desire.

Believing is a capacity of mind—and we have perhaps already begun to discover how limited mind can be.

The Buddha Way, as experienced by Gautama, is along a path of continually giving up beliefs when they cease to be useful or are seen to be false, of keeping the mind flexible—so that, gradually, its arbitrary concepts cease to be the dominant dictators of our lives.

*

You may not know exactly who is suffering, but question yourself: What is the essence of this mind? Think only of this. You will need no more. Covet nothing. Your end which is endless is as a snowflake dissolving in the pure air . . .

How can I "believe" in a snowflake's end?
Or
How can I believe in a snowflake?

Four

One day a fifty-year-old student of enlightenment said to the master, Shinkan: "I have studied the Tendai school of thought since I was a little boy, but one thing in it I cannot understand. Tendai claims that even the grass and trees will become enlightened. To me this seems very strange."

"Of what use is it to discuss how trees and grass become enlightened?" asked Shinkan. "The question is how yourself can become so. Did you ever consider that?"

"I never thought of it in that way," marvelled the old man.

"Then go home and think it over," finished Shinkan.

Zen story

*

How you or I can become enlightened may seem an unlikely subject for consideration, but it is at the very heart of Gautama's message to us.

One of the prime difficulties experienced by any serious "seeker after Truth" through the religious life is that he or she—the aspirant—very soon comes up against the *belief* that the founder of the particular religion under scrutiny is or was in some way superhuman—and therefore not like us.

Although Gautama may have been a mortal man—as it is suggested were Jesus, Abraham, Mohammed and all the other great religious founders—he was nevertheless a "divine creation" and it would be foolish, if not sacreligious (profane) to think of him as being just simply an ordinary man.

This belief is both a help and a terrible hindrance on our path to enlightenment.

54

It is a help in precisely the same way that a pattern is a help to a tailor, a set of plans to an architect, or a blueprint to a scientist. It gives us, in other words, a structure on which to build, an ideal to aim for and an idea of what we should strive to emulate.

The hindrance is that we rarely question *what* it is we are building, *why* it is that we are aiming for the ideal nor *how* it is that we should emulate it.

We may seek to fashion our lives on the life of another "human being"—whom we have never seen, nor never heard speak—but whom we only know about through the stories, the *reported* words and the *reported* deeds. Thus our pattern or blueprint is at the very best, second-hand!

It would be hard enough for me to try and live as you ... even if I had you constantly in the room with me, so that I could copy you. But, if I have never met you ...?

And how would I copy you?

I certainly couldn't change myself physically—so that I was a replica of you. If you're tall and I'm short ... there is no way that I'm going to get tall.

So, physically I will remain recognizably me.

Mentally I may adopt many of your ideas and attitudes. I may learn to like the things that you like and to dislike the things that you do not like. I may come to express myself in the way that you express yourself ... I may, in fact, intellectually and emotionally become imbued with your ideas, opinions and beliefs. This is seen to happen constantly during the course of our lives. It begins within the family environment, continues through the days of our schooling and does not stop when we take our place in the adult world; the very friends that we choose enforce and enhance our already crystallized ideas about ourselves and the world we live in.

Think about it: Is there any single opinion or belief that you can call entirely your own; that was not in some degree acquired from someone else?

So yes—mentally I can become like you.

But is that true, or is it only superficial? Can I see through your eyes? Can I hear through your ears? Can I share your actual feelings? I wonder to what extent I can ever be like you mentally? For to be like you mentally I would have to take and use your mind.

So, physically and mentally, however much I may wish to change myself I am bound to the individual body and the individual mind with which I started off in the samsaric world.

The religious life speaks also of the "spirit" of a man—and a religious aspirant, reading the above will already be impatiently claiming that the point is being missed. The point being? That it is "spiritually" that we seek to emulate our chosen master, religious founder or whatever. We are asked to believe that he is—or was— "perfect".

This idea of a perfect human being is very far reaching.

If there are perfect human beings—then that automatically allows that there are also "imperfect" ones. And, in the religious context, the religious founder is always claimed by his disciples to be perfect and it is this perfection that should be striven for.

Thus the founder—Gautama, Jesus, Mohammed . . . whoever— is "perfect" and we, all the rest of us—you and me—are "imperfect". (And, although we need not go into it here—this concept is further complicated by there apparently being degrees of imperfection; from the "evil-doer" right up to the "saint".)

But what is a "perfect" human being?

What makes him perfect?

Why should he be perfect—when we are not?

Was he born perfect—or did he attain perfection?

If he was born perfect—then are not all newly-born babies perfect? Were not you perfect once? Was not I perfect once?

What happened then? Did we lose our perfection—and did he, somehow, maintain his?

Or:

If he attained perfection through his life—then is it not also possible for you to attain this perfection; is it not possible for me to attain this perfection?

56

It all depends upon what is meant by perfect and perfection.

If the creation is the mystical expression of some unseen deity (as many religions suggest) then why, one wonders, should there be any such thing as imperfection? Wouldn't it have been easier and more beneficial to have left imperfection out of the blueprint?

What is imperfection?

Can you have an imperfect dawn? An imperfect sound? Can you have imperfect light, imperfect scents, imperfect tastes, imperfect feelings?

Do not all such ideas of imperfection depend upon a vague blueprint, already established in mind, of what perfect is?

Where, one wonders, did that idea come from?

Furthermore, if I am an imperfect being, I am only so in comparison with some other being who is generally accepted—or accepted by me—as being perfect.

But perfect in what respect? How they behave? How they look? How they speak? How they feel?

It is very natural that we should want to know all that we can about such a person—for, not only are we supposed to be striving to emulate them, but also they in turn are showing us up as being less than perfect ourselves.

And so, where possible, we try to discover the "history" of such a person.

*

History ... the record of a series of events ... Gautama's history ...

His story.

Gautama's story.

The story of Gautama's life, as we read it twenty-five centuries after his death, is generally accepted as being part fact and part legend. And there is little enough of it anyway. Commentators have suggested that one reason for this may be that what Gautama *did* was considered to be of little importance compared with what he *said*.

(Are we then judged by what we *say* rather than what we *do*? Or do we only express ourselves in the light of our behaviour?)

Whatever the reasons for our having but a sketch of the man's life, the salient events that we are told about have an extraordinary potency if we view them in a certain way.

*

Ordinarily, and as commonly represented, I will consider Gautama as any other historical figure. I will relate him to my view and comprehension of historical fact.

And so I can readily accept that as a man he was born, lived about eighty years, and died; and furthermore, that all this happened a long time ago. (Here the comprehension is vague because I am used to conducting my everyday life within the range of minutes, hours and days. My grasp of time duration begins to become more tenuous as I start to measure and locate events at distances of weeks, months and years. By the time I am trying to comprehend centuries and millennia time has extended to durations which I cannot really accommodate because they are well beyond the limits of my experience.)

Once I *believe* in duration of passing time and in the historical view of life, I am committed to a particular way of structuring my thought and thus to a particular view of events which conditions my comprehension of everything that happens. For I will always try to relate and order my observations in logical *sequence*. And then I will base my concepts and beliefs on the assumed structure. For example, I think of birth as a beginning and death as an ending. Once conditioned to that view, it is hard to accommodate the possibility that birth is an ending and death a beginning; or, even harder, that time does not "pass" at all, and that birth-death is the dual aspect of one simultaneous and timeless event. (When I am "here" there is a "there"; but when I am "there", the "here" becomes the "there" and the "there" becomes "here". "Here" and "there"— both are "everywhere", simultaneously).

Being committed to a finite, historical, sequential view causes

58

considerable complications and difficulty. (As, for example, we have touched on earlier in considering how the mind conceives of "former lives", how it stalls when it tries to get back "before the beginning" or beyond "after the end", and how it has to settle for an indefinable "first cause" to which it gives the name "God" or whatever.)

Due to my learning—based entirely on the fundamental idea that "I" am this body—I seem to have no option but to think in terms of cause followed by effect, the birth-life-death sequence and a "thousand" other logical orders and laws, always in terms of the passing time concept of past-present-future.

It is not easy at first to see the full power and effect of this conditioning. Once we are caught, there would seem no escape. It literally rules the mind like a tyrant. We are totally bound and move inexorably along with it to the "precipice" of death as extinction. So many of the attempted answers to our profound questions are unsatisfactory in its terms; so many of our experiences cannot be convincingly explained.

Take for example the different "people" that each of us has been, historically. We must all have experienced the embarrassing situation of "baby-stories" being told about us. Is the "me" that listens to such stories now in any way a *result* of the baby being talked about? Sequentially the answer may be "yes"—but it is certainly hard to see it psychologically and intellectually. This becomes more pressingly acute as a problem when we consider "past deeds". To what extent is the "me" today responsible for actions, decisions, deeds . . . taken by a "me" of possibly many years ago? "I have changed" I may say—but the deed is there—stuck in my "history", inextinguishable. If, to take an extreme example, I was a murderer *then* . . . am I still a murderer *now*? (The very act of murdering may have had such a shattering effect on me that since then I may have utterly changed my "life style" and I may now be a devoted aspirant after Truth . . . in fact, the very act of murdering *could* be the vital step on my path to *enlightenment*.)

In this example once again we are touching on the concept of *karma* and it is interesting to note that in the Vedantic tradition—

from whence stemmed what we now call the Hindu religion (and, incidentally, the very tradition that we may assume Gautama was first introduced to)—a constant injunction in the Upanishads (the "sacred songs" of the Vedas) is:

... *remember past deeds. Mind! remember past deeds: remember, Mind! remember.*

But, remember *how*? As a sequential series of events that all happened to one me? Or as a series of "me's" that are all remembered by one mind?

*

However, as far as Gautama and Buddhism are concerned, we can if we wish settle for history's account. We can *learn* of a series of events that happened "a long time ago"; we can *learn* what Gautama is reported to have done and said; we can *learn* what happened afterwards—the subsequent interpretations of what he meant, the spread of Buddhism and of the multitude of "genuine" and "suspect" doctrines, beliefs, practices and rituals. And we can believe or not believe. We can take it or leave it—as if it was and is "something" *separate* from us which we can pick up or put aside according to whether *we* happen to find it sympathetic or alien. In short we can treat it as just another interesting or boring occupation.

Such is the consequence of our conditioning—a separation and then accepting and rejecting, as if such things *exist in their own right* for us to espouse or dispose of at will.

Can that *really* be the sense of it?

Supposing there was a totally other way of viewing it which had nothing to do with our arbitrary prejudices, whims and fancies?

Supposing we consider the idea that the process of development—innocent baby, learning about the world, thinking being separate from the world, thinking that life and will are ours, believing in the sequence of passing time—is a universal, inevitable, and in terms of survival, a practical and useful process, but that it is not the *only* development? Furthermore, that it may only be a crude and pre-

60

liminary step in the unfolding of man's potential? Could it not be that if this initial process does remain the only way of viewing life then there comes a time, its usefulness outlived, when it becomes a positive hindrance and limitation, even causing an "illness" of mind?

Just as a baby has to leave the womb, the chick break out of the egg, the son leave the home, so might we not have to give up and disband structures of thinking which are past their usefulness? Can we make the leap from the idea that Buddhism is a religion that we can learn about and accept or reject, to the transcendent perspective which reveals that, language and labels apart, if we are searching for Truth then we are "Buddhist" and potentially "Buddha"?

*

Wordiness and intellection—
The more with them, the further astray we go;
Away therefore with wordiness and intellection,
And there is no place where we cannot pass freely.

When we return to the root, we gain the meaning;
When we pursue external objects we lose the reason.
The moment we are enlightened within,
We go beyond the voidness of a world confronting us.

Transformations going on in an empty world which confronts us
Appear real all because of ignorance:
Try not to seek after the true,
Only cease to cherish opinions . . .

(SENG-TS'AN, *On Believing in Mind*)

*

How can we develop such a perspective?
Through the "here-and-now".
Experience . . . for each of us, for you and for me . . . *is* here and now . . . no time and nowhere else.

61

Let us forget history for a moment.

Let us instead try to comprehend Gautama's existence itself and put aside the development of what is now called Buddhism. "Buddhism", as the name of a religion, is only a label that has been tied for convenience on a massive collection of other men's ideas, beliefs, interpretations, opinions, doctrines, practices and rituals . . . recorded through history.

Let us see, if we can, what elements of his story help us, here and now, in our own experience.

Assuming that the man Gautama existed (and always bearing in mind that it doesn't really matter if he did or not) we hear the story of his life. And, after certain events in that life, we hear that he achieved "enlightenment" and became "Buddha".

If we say that he became *a* Buddha or *the* Buddha—what happens?

Immediately we conceive of "Buddha" as an object located in time and space . . .

But, as "enlightenment" suggests, Gautama, the historical figure, achieved an extraordinary realization or experienced a "heightened", exceptional, out-of-the-ordinary state of mind.

It is not going to be easy to convey or comprehend what such an experience might be like (unless we can achieve and experience such a state ourselves) for the words will probably fail us but, if we accept the evidence, then he undoubtedly saw a totally different perspective or view of the human condition and its purpose. So "illuminated" and convinced was he by this insight that he spent the rest of his life teaching others how they might see it also, for he realized that it was "the Way" out of *dukkha*.

There is no doubt that those who came into contact with him at the time were aware that Gautama was discovering something vitally important and naturally wanted to know and experience it themselves. There is no human power like the attraction of someone who *knows* for the person who wants to know . . . unless it be the object of *love* for the one who needs to love.

And naturally the disciple or lover elevates the teacher or the loved one to divine and immaculate proportions in his mind, and surrenders to devotion and even worship. The legacy of this reputation lingers on through time and when we hear tell of a man of such wisdom and stature, we think of *a* person who achieved this wisdom in time *past*.

But if we focus on the idea that "Buddha" is the name that would be given to *any* man who *achieves* such an exceptional "state of mind", then the confusions and obscurities of history dissolve.

Relieved of trying to comprehend what Gautama was or what Buddhism was or is, we may simply concentrate here and now on what the "Buddha-experience" *is* . . . in the sense that we may here and now experience what Gautama experienced thousands of years ago.

Gautama experienced a state of mind that in the language of his place and time was called "Buddha".

No matter what name we may choose to give it today, whoever and wherever we are, we may also experience that same "enlightenment"—a truer, profounder, wiser perspective and insight on the human condition and purpose—if we wish to do so.

You and I may achieve "Buddha-hood".

I am Buddha in potential.

You are Buddha in potential.

"But", the logical, sequential mind will object, "if it is in potential and I do not *yet* know it, then I can only realize it in the future."

Such is our bondage of thinking in sequence.

The alternative view (which may not be really an alternative but the "real" view), as we have suggested, sees sequence as an illusion.

Once we really see who and what we are, it will be as though what we thought we were never existed! The former lives dissolve as a dream vanishes in the immediacy of waking.

*

And so . . .

When I think I am "here", I create a "there"—where I am not. But then I realize that when I am "there", that "there" becomes

63

"here"—and the "here" becomes "there". Therefore all "heres" are "there", and vice versa. Both "here" and "there" are the same —when I am "everywhere".

When I think I am not Buddha, I create a "Buddha". When I realize Buddha, I realize that I am Buddha thinking I was not Buddha. In reality, there is never a time when I am not Buddha.

*

This may all seem complicated and exasperating to us—but never mind! We have only begun to explore what Gautama called "the Path" or "the Way" and maybe it will help us to gain confidence in the idea that there may be a totally different way of understanding the nature of our existence to that which we have been accustomed to through our early learning and belief.

*

"This is myself and this is another."
Be free of this bond which encompasses you about,
And your own self is thereby released.
Do not err in this matter of self and other.
Everything is Buddha without exception.
Here is that immaculate and final stage,
Where thought is pure in its true nature.

(From SARAHA'S *Treasury of Songs*)

*

And so we will continue to look at Gautama's life not in terms of the historical man who became "a Buddha" but in terms of his life and experience in the light of our own.

He was born into existence, *samsara.*

We are born into existence, *samsara.*

Let us continue from that common starting point,

It is said that Gautama was born a "prince".

Never mind for our purpose here what worldly connotations that may have. In those terms very few of us are princes. But "prince", as a word, derives from Latin words meaning "first" (*primus*) and "to take" (*capere*). And from the word "prince" we form such words as "principal" and "principle" with their connotations of fundamental source, prime importance, chief law, first premise on which to base truth . . . and so on.

To ourselves, we are all born "princes".

"I" am born.

"I" is the principal; the principle upon which will be based what "I" become, namely "me".

If you like, you are born as a "prince" in your "kingdom"— your new physical existence. And, of course, that carries the implications that eventually you will be "king", the ruler of that "kingdom".

So, in the early days, "prince" best describes the essential "you" who needs to learn much about the world before becoming wise enough to rule your own life.

*

Gautama is born into a wealthy, powerful and privileged family. Very few of us have that childhood situation . . . in the world's terms.

But as human beings—as distinct from dogs, snakes, trees, stones or whatever—do we not find ourselves heirs to extraordinary wealth, power and privilege? If we discount, for the purpose of this discussion, the economic poverty and deprivation brought about in the world through *man's own* mismanagement and greed, then the life principle ("I") born into the species "man" receives a wealth of resources and potential, mental powers of knowledge and communication and a privileged status way above those of the other creatures with whom he shares this planet, "earth".

In this sense you and I are born into a "family" of incomparable wealth, power and privilege. How we may use this in competition with others is another matter altogether—but is it not significant that we rarely, if ever, consider ourselves fortunate and richly blessed simply in that each of us has been born "a human being"? We do *not* consider in this way because once again we are up against

C*   65

the limitations of *mind* which cannot conceive of itself as part of a whole ("life") but believes itself to be individual, separate and belonging only to "me". The concept of a "universal mind" is as impossible for our "individual mind" to comprehend as is the concept of a "universal life force" reaching eternally *before* "birth" and *after* "death".

*

I have recognized the deepest truth, which is sublime and peace-giving, but difficult to understand; for most men move in a sphere of worldly interests and find their delight in worldly desires. The world-ling will not understand the doctrine, for to him there is happiness in selfhood only, and the bliss that lies in a complete surrender to truth is unintelligible to him. He will call resignation what to the enlightened mind is the purest joy. He will see annihilation where the perfected one finds immortality. He will regard as death what the conqueror of self knows to be life everlasting. The truth remains hidden from him who is in the bondage of hate and desire. Nirvana remains incomprehensible to the vulgar whose minds are beclouded with worldly interests.

(*Sayings of Buddha*)

*

It is then related that Gautama lived a luxurious and protected life in "his father's palace" until almost thirty years of age. During this time he married and had a son; otherwise his life was hedonistic in the extreme, a continual self-indulgence in all manner of sensual appetite.

By all accounts Gautama was an extremely intelligent boy and it is stretching credibility to suppose that during all that time he did not learn anything of the world outside or hear about such afflictions as disease, old-age and death.

Perhaps we may surmise that his life in the "palace" was secluded or protected to the extent that he never had first-hand *experience* of observing these afflictions and that therefore they did not worry him.

66

Or, when we look for the parallel in our own experience, it may be that although he may have known about and observed such afflictions, the full import of them *in relation to himself* did not strike him.

During our childhood we do observe such afflictions and get to know about them but we are curiously protected from their significance *to us*. Children take such things mainly as a matter of course, do not trouble about them, and get on with their own play and concerns (their "self-indulgence"). It is only when we start to *become aware of ourselves* in relation to the world outside our home and family, and begin to consider the long-term future of our lives, that the full import of these things potentially being *our* own afflictions may seriously assail us so that the anxiety and horror of it actively disturbs our minds.

Even then we may continue to be "protected" from the repercussions in many ways. Mentally we may be able to persuade ourselves that "it won't happen to me . . . not yet anyway"; or we manage to explain and compensate with appropriate beliefs, especially the doctrines of our religious conditioning—"Poverty and disease are punishment for stupidity and wickedness" or "After I die, I will go to paradise or heaven . . . if I am 'good' now," and so on.

And we may be able to keep this up for many years—even past the age of marriage and parenthood—and continue with striving for our share of the world's pleasures regardless. But then, one day, possibly through the shock of some personal confrontation, the full significance does strike us . . . and anxiety and even horror fill the mind.

In this way, doesn't our story parallel that of Gautama's?

*

What happens next?

Gautama, after his first shock of confrontation, began to question. We also, having once awoken to our physical vulnerability, may well begin to question the causes of the afflictions, why we

67

should have to suffer them and whether they are avoidable—and if they are not, then how we may deal with them or overcome them.

We may be so impressed and affected by this "awakening" (which may be sudden or gradual) that our whole life begins to change. It is a very definite point in our "growing up" and the way in which we deal with it very much colours our thoughts and actions from then onwards.

However, we are unlikely to take such drastic steps as Gautama apparently did—if we read his story literally. We will not immediately swing our life-style and attitudes to the opposite extreme . . . shunning the opposite sex, being filled with pity for all living things, longing for solitude, giving up all self-indulgence and pleasure seeking, rejecting domestic life, becoming a celibate ascetic . . . But we may begin to entertain such thoughts and to act on them to a degree. Especially during adolescence we are likely to experience the friction and discomfort of such thoughts as they come into opposition with what we are used to. Our old "protected" life of childhood is now felt both as a comfort and a restriction. We want to be "worthy"—but we do not know what that means. We want to explore and find the answers for ourselves but we do not know how to. So though we may not necessarily, literally and physically, take revolutionary action, mentally we experience hate alongside love in our relationship with parents, family, the opposite sex, friends; we experience pity and the desire to help our fellow men and, at the same time, the temptation to pursue pleasure and gain for ourselves; we feel the need for seclusion and privacy alongside our gregariousness; we are secure within the family and yet we begin to know that we will have to go out into the world and establish independence; we know perhaps the urge, after over-indulgence in sensual appetite, to restore the balance by acts of self-deprivation and sacrifice.

And so, if we have a sense of recognition in the above commentary, we may feel ourselves closer to and in sympathy with Gautama's story and we may be the more prepared to follow what happens next—because, if we know something of the common discomfort and conflict and we are told that Gautama found "the Way" to resolve it . . . then we will certainly want to know what it was that he discovered.

*

In this chapter, we the authors, could be charged by you, the reader, with having taken the reported historical aspect of Gautama's early years and re-presented it in a way that will, presumably, enforce *our* particular view.

And this, of course, would be fair comment.

However, two essential observations would arise out of such a criticism.

Firstly, *all* communication—whether it be through speech or the written word—can only be from the viewpoint of the author (or, in this case, the authors). There is no book written that does not depend upon the vision of the writer. The whole canon of the "Buddhist scriptures" being, as they are, the reports by *others* of what Gautama did and said—are dependent upon the particular view of those who did the reporting. Just consider, if you were now to assess what all the pages of this book were trying to say . . . would you come up with the same summary as that of another person who has read the book?

Here again, *karma*—in its role of selector of that which is relevant to the individual—may be seen at work.

We will each of us respond in a way peculiar and particular to our own persuasions. We will each of us "view the world and all things in it" from the particular stand-point of *our* experience of the world and all that happens to us. In this way "feawe"—as coined in chapter one—not being in our experience, will be either described verbatim and without any particular commitment, or will be forgotten—and therefore ignored and left out of our assessment. *Or* it will be *re-presented* by us—because, although we have not experienced it as such, it nevertheless evoked a recognition in us of some thing; in other words, it "made a point".

Thus *our* view is related to *your* view through the recognition of a mutually similar experience.

Secondly it should be mentioned that in the scriptures the bare bones of Gautama's first years are much overlaid with magical and mystical legend (which, in a sense, justifies our treatment and use of them here—because such "embroidery" detracts from the ability to take them too literally in the historical sense and substantiates the need to "read" them as allegoric and symbolic).

Among such mystical and magical ingredients (with all the echoes of other religious traditions) we may read that:

Gautama's mother, who resembled the goddess Maya, had a strange vision or dream before conceiving him;

that her conception was "without defilement";

that she suffered no discomfort during pregnancy;

that Gautama was miraculously born "out of her side";

that Gautama immediately walked;

and that, after his birth, a "wise man" or seer came unannounced to the palace and, having "read the signs", prophesied that the baby would grow up to become one who would "proclaim the path of salvation".

Such incidents, which are clearly not in our experience in mundane terms, must indicate that we should consider Gautama's story not simply as the history of a particular man but as representing the universal and timeless inspiration, nature and purpose invested in and evolving out of Man—the story of the selfhood in each of us.

*

The "symbolic description" is a device much employed in religious teaching for two very good reasons:

Firstly it is a way of describing ideas that are "beyond" the capabilities of ordinary mind—confined as it is to sequential reasoning and the finite world.

Secondly a symbol only *means* what it does to the individual *now* —in other words it has no meaning other than that which the recipient invests it with. So the understanding of the symbolic, the magical, the mystical, ingredient reminds us not to think of Gautama's story as separated from us by passing time nor as happening in logical sequence. Gautama's story only is *now* as we hear it and as each of us recognizes it for *ourselves*.

The whole story is *now*. We are enacting it *now*.

How can it ever be otherwise?

If you are not hearing the story *now*—where is the story for *you*?

If you are hearing the story *now*—how can the story belong to the historic past?

Because of sequential thinking and the way we write, we have to set the story down in a long line of letters. But, once read, it is all contained as a complete story in memory. It is whole and immediately there if we recall it—but it will take a space and time to relate it to someone else. To relate it we will employ the device—just as we do on this page—of a series of words, evolving a series of events, following a logical order, travelling "through time".

But—is that how it, or any story, is contained in your mind?

In any given moment we may be experiencing any single aspect of the story; we may be innocent, learning, believing, understanding, worried, horrified, self-indulgent, going "out" to someone, withdrawing, realizing, accepting, rejecting, hating, loving, dying . . .

It all happens *now* . . .

We may read of it happening to Gautama—but who is "Gautama"? How can we begin to understand his story and his experience—if we have not already got the story and the experiences somewhere within our own "spiritual", "enlivened", "creational" psyche? To recognize means simply to "know again" . . . does the "unknown" make any impression upon us? How can it? How can I know again what I have never known?

It all happens *now* . . .

It all revolves in an eternal cycle around the "centre" . . . Buddha.

*

A centre point is dimensionless and therefore invisible and intangible.

Describe that point . . . and there is a centre point within the point . . . describe that point . . . and there is a centre deep within that.

As a centre it is anywhere and everywhere.

For us the cycle of life experience is like marking out the circumference of the circle . . . it (the circumference) serves only to define and prove the centre.

All experience is *now* . . . all events—the murder in the past, the baby-stories, the adolescent frictions . . . all points on the circumference, all equidistant from the eternal, motionless centre . . . Buddha.

"Of what use is it to discuss how trees and grass become enlightened? The question is how you yourself can become so. Did you ever consider that? . . .

Then go home and think it over . . ."

*

Who is *Buddha*?
Where is *Buddha*?
What is *Buddha*?

Who am I?

*

He is not seen to come,
Nor known to stay or go;
As signless and motionless the supreme Lord is known.

(From SARAHA'S *Treasury of Songs*)

AN INTERVAL

And so we have reached a point which is roughly halfway through the book. And, as with any journey—where rests along the way are advisable if one is to reach one's destination in a fit and healthy state and not exhausted—so here let us rest for a few moments and consider the ground that we have already covered, the sights we have seen.

You, the reader, and we, the authors, will probably never meet —and yet we are sharing a mutual event within the pages of this book. This is not to suggest that you are necessarily responding to and agreeing with the *ideas* that we are transmitting—but certainly you are reading the words here on this page in precisely the way that we are reading the words . . . the words are neutral, made up of a certain number of letters in a certain order; that is all. The *meaning* that the words contain *cannot* be in those letters and in that sequential placing of those letters—can it?

Where is the *meaning*?

The meaning is up to each of us. The meaning is what is going on in the mind of each of us.

The words are immovable, neutral, frozen and dead here on the page. Just look at them:

WORD   MEANING   PAGE

Having been set down, they are there for as long as the book remains.

They are the *event*, which we are sharing.

They are not the *experience* of the *event*. That cannot be shared. That belongs to each of us individually.

73

When you started reading this book there was, no doubt, the idea that, if the book was of interest to you, you would read it to the end. Thus the *end* of the book was your "destination" when you *began* the book.

All well and good; but, having reached your destination will you be any different, will you be changed?

In sequential appreciation you will be a little older—for time will have "passed".

But, apart from that, will there be any change?

Mentally you may have adopted new ideas—if so, will you have borrowed them from us, the authors? Certainly the ideas will have come to you *through* the words that we are now setting down on these pages.

Who then owns the ideas? Are they "yours", or are they "ours"? Could not "our" ideas have stimulated quite other ideas which in turn are "your" ideas?

Who owns the ideas?

And perhaps, along the way—while reading this book—you will all of a sudden, or very very gradually, but effectively all of a *sudden* . . . be enlightened . . .

But—who is "enlightened"?

You?

Who has enlightened you?

Certainly not *us*, the authors, nor these words on the page.

Your moment of enlightenment—your "flash of the light of Truth"—comes only *through you.*

BUDDHA enlightens . . . BUDDHA.

From that moment—*now* when it happens—your view of the world will be entirely changed; it will never be the same again.

And why else are you reading this book? What point is there in reading—or doing—anything, save that through the reading, or through the doing, there may be this moment of change, this light, this inexpressible re-birth?

To put it another way:

We the authors started writing this book and our destination is the end of this book. We know where we are heading—the last page!

But the last page is as meaningless as the first page . . . before the first word on the first page there was a *space*, just paper with nothing on it; after the last word on the last page there will be a *space*, just paper with nothing on it. . .

Our destination will be where we begin.

The "end" is the "beginning".

Only the journey is important.

Through what we *see* on the journey, how we *experience* the journey, how we *live* the journey, we will be prepared for reaching that final space and *knowing* it for the first time.

The *space* will not have changed—*we* will have changed . . . not by reaching our destination—but . . . by making the journey.

*

So, let us rest before continuing with this book, with this journey, with this experience.

Rest? How?

Sleep? Do something else? Read something else?

How do we rest?

The *centre* is always at rest.

The *circumference* moves and turns.

Find the *centre* . . .

Thus I have heard

Paradoxical though it may seem: There is a path to walk on, there is walking being done, but there is no traveller. There are deeds being done, but there is no doer. There is a blowing of the air, but there is no wind that does the blowing. The thought of self is an error and all existences are as hollow as the plantain tree and as empty as twirling water bubbles.

Therefore as there is no self, there is no transmigration of a self; but there are deeds and the continued effect of deeds. There is a rebirth of karma; there is reincarnation. This rebirth, this reincarnation, this re-appearance of the conformations is continuous and depends on the law of cause and effect. Just as a seal is impressed upon wax reproducing the configurations of its device, so the thoughts of men, their characters, their aspirations are impressed upon others in continuous transference and continue their karma, and good deeds will continue in blessings while bad deeds will continue in curses.

The body is a compound of perishable organs. It is subject to decay; we should attend to its needs without being attached to it, or loving it. The body is like a machine, and there is no self in it that makes it walk or act, but the thoughts of it, as the windy elements, cause the machine to work. The body moves about like a cart . . .

Thus have I heard

Since there is no self, there can not be any after life of a self. Therefore abandon all thought of self. But since there are deeds and since deeds continue, be careful with your deeds. All beings have karma as their portion: *They are heirs of their karma: They are sprung from their karma: Their karma is their kinsman: Their karma is their refuge: karma allots beings to meanness or to greatness.*

The rational nature of man is a spark of the true light; it is the first step on the upward road. But new births are required to insure an ascent to the summit of existence, the enlightenment of mind and heart, where the immeasurable light of moral comprehension is gained which is the source of all righteousness. Having attained this higher birth, I have found the truth and have taught you the noble path that leads to the city of peace. I have shown you the way to the lake of ambrosia, which washes away all evil desire. I have given you the refreshing drink called the perception of truth, and he who drinks of it becomes free from excitement, passion and wrong-doing.

The very gods envy the bliss of him who has escaped from the floods of passion and has climbed the shores of Nirvana. His heart is cleansed from all defilement and free from all illusion. He is like unto the lotus which grows in the water, yet not a drop of water adheres to its petals. The man who walks in the noble path lives in the world, and yet his heart is not defiled by worldly desires.

He who does not see the four noble truths, he who does not understand the three characteristics and has not grounded himself in the uncreate, has still a long path to traverse; by repeated births through the desert of ignorance with its mirages of illusion, and through the morass of wrong. But now that you have gained comprehension, the cause of further migrations and aberrations is removed. The goal is reached. The craving of selfishness is destroyed, and the truth is attained. This is true deliverance; this is salvation; this is heaven and the bliss of a life immortal . . .

(*Sayings of Buddha*)

. . . the *centre* must be there for the *circumference* to be there.

Without a *centre* there can be no *circumference*.

Thus the centre *is* always.

It is everywhere and anywhere.

There is no *movement* without *rest*.

Movement serves only to define and prove *rest*.

In every action, there is rest.

Without rest—the still, silent, *centre*—there can be no movement, sound or circumference.

By all means, when we make a journey, let us take our "moments of rest".

By all means, as we continue with this book, let us be mindful—we the authors and you the reader—that our destination is a space, that our beginning was a space . . . and that between each word there is space, between each letter of each word there is space, within each letter there is space.

What is a letter—but a shape, defining a space?

The *rest* is *space*: The *space* is the *centre*.

Where we "began" is where we "are" is where we will "end".

Paradoxical though it may seem: There is a book to write, there is writing being done, but there is no author . . .

Paradoxical though it may seem: There is a book to read, there is reading being done, but there is no reader . . .

Paradoxical though it may seem: There is a path to walk on, there is walking being done, but there is no traveller . . .

Five

Nan-in, a Japanese master during the Meiji era received a university professor who came to enquire about Zen.

Nan-in served tea. He poured his visitor's cup full, and then kept on pouring.

The professor watched the overflow until he could no longer restrain himself. "It is overfull. No more will go in!"

"Like this cup," Nan-in said, "you are full of your own opinions and speculations. How can I show you Zen unless you first empty your cup?"

Zen story

*

The impact on Gautama of realizing the inevitable decline, decay and demise of the human body was such that it changed his whole outlook on life.

We all may recognize how, when we begin to emerge from the "protection" of our childhood world, we also are impressed by certain aspects of the "reality" of life. We begin to become "adult"; and part and parcel of becoming adult is that we are deeply impressed by realizations which did not trouble us as children. Surely among the most significant of these realizations is when it dawns upon us that *we ourselves* are actually destined to become old and die.

For Gautama—as usually with us—such realizations raise questions and cause concern in the mind.

We "awaken" to all kinds of challenge which we attempt to meet with what mental resources we have. There are only two possibilities; and we have to adopt one or the other because such questions are felt as a threat to happiness and it is happiness that we want above all else. One way is to suppress and ignore the questions; the alternative is to try to find answers. Perhaps, from time to time over the passing days and years we will do both; it will depend on our natures and circumstances.

As far as Gautama is concerned, his nature dictated that he determined to find the answers at all costs . . . and he was prepared to give up anything and everything to search for the key to lasting happiness.

*

Gautama—if we may presume to interpret what he is recorded to have said and done—reacted passionately against his erstwhile life of luxury and security as a prince in his father's palace.

He is said to have reasoned something like this:

If I have lived my life so far in pursuing that which is bound eventually to pass away, what sense is there in that? How can I continue to rely for my happiness on that which cannot last?

Why do I, who am subject to birth, decay and death, look for my happiness and fulfilment in that which is also subject to such a fate?

Should I not, after realizing how all things in the world are transitory, seek after that which does not pass away?

Is it possible that there is that which is not subject to birth, suffering, disease, illness, decay and death? Is there that which is unborn, invulnerable, ageless and does not die?

Having reasoned thus, Gautama found himself unable any longer to take pleasure and delight in the "sense-objects" around him. His sense of contentment disappeared and he could not regain a feeling of security.

He is reported as saying:

"I find neither peace nor contentment, and enjoyment is quite out of the question—for the world looks to me as if ablaze with an all-consuming fire. If a man has once grasped that death is quite inevitable, and if nevertheless greed arises in his heart, then he must surely have an iron will not to weep in this great danger, but to enjoy it."

*

If we continue to draw a parallel with our own experience we may not literally give up our childhood pleasures and pursuits overnight, but, inevitably, as the significance of adult life dawns on us, we will begin to turn away from and abandon our childhood dreams and concerns.

We will "put away childish things".

Gautama, faced with the realization of the uselessness of his princely life, was forced to consider what he should do. He decided to go "to the forest", to find solitude—to find peace and quiet where he could think it out for himself.

In just such a way we may contemplate the problems of life as we walk alone in the countryside or by the sea, in the privacy of our own room, as we lie awake in bed at night . . .

*

Gautama found that he loved the countryside and its beauty but that the suffering of the men and the creatures he observed in it filled him with a great sadness.

He sat in a secluded place and contemplated the changing of all things—their coming into existence, their growth, their fullness, their withering and their decay and final destruction. The realization of the universality of this fate calmed his mind and filled him with compassion. He realized further that in his own fear of decay and death he had ignored the fact that it was inexorably the fate of all things; and that in this personal disquiet he was at one with the suffering and the disquiet of all things, *whether they were aware of it or not*. And, through this realization he saw that there was no sense or use in self-concern. Why think of it and harbour it as a personal worry? What he needed to understand was not just for himself but also for the whole of creation. His own fate was the fate of all.

This, no doubt after much disciplined and precise contemplatio n,

81

instilled in him a quiet detachment and a clarity of mind which opened his heart to the universal quest and to a compassion which could not be withheld from any living creature.

*

Again we may see a parallel with our own developing experience.

Might we have a glimpse of the triviality and uselessness of our own self-concern and simultaneously feel stirred by the realization that we are all together in the human predicament? And may we be moved by the open-hearted view that whatever abilities we have could be used as a contribution to the universal search for truth and happiness?

If I may discover "that" which is unborn, changeless, ageless and immortal, then "that" will not be for "me" . . . for I am born and I change, I age and I die.

"That" will be the same unborn, changeless, ageless, and immortal for all created things in their totality . . . which includes "me".

*

When I have passed away and can no longer address you and edify your minds with religious discourse, select from among you men of good family and education to preach the truth in my stead. And let those men be invested with the robes of the Perfect One, let them enter into his abode, and occupy his pulpit.

The robe of the Perfect One is sublime forebearance and patience. His abode is charity and love of all beings. His pulpit is the comprehension of the good law: its eternal truth, and its daily lesson for all men.

(*Sayings of Buddha*)

*

In this clarity of mind and opening of the heart, Gautama is said to have received the *dharma*.

Dharma is a word representing one of those concepts whose very nature—if it can even be said to have a nature—defies definition. For anything which is conceivable and definable by the thinking mind is not *dharma*.

There are many indications of *dharma* in the scriptures and all manner of meanings, sometimes mutually contradictory, are given to it. It requires a very subtle mental perception but we must make an effort to convey something of its "nature".

Dharma could be said to relate to the truth or reality of what *is*.

It is that which is left when all untruth and falsity is removed from the deluded mind.

It is that which is self-evident to the fully conscious mind when all discursive thinking and imagining has ceased.

It is the virtue, justice, order and rule which upholds all creation.

It is under-standing the "is-ness", the universal being of all things as a unified whole.

It is the intuitive or wordless cognition of absolute unity.

It is the undeniable knowledge born of actual experience at the profoundest levels of mind perception.

It is the unqualified consciousness wherein all forms exist.

The *dharma* is not "something" that was or will be; *it is what is —now*.

It is in this respect that Gautama, as Buddha, is said to have taught the *dharma*; that is to say, not as a doctrine to be *believed* but as an *understanding* to be earned and experienced.

*

It is as if we, as we emerge into an independent and adult life, face an unknown world . . . a world which will teach us all that we need to know, providing only that we do not separate ourselves off from it through obsessive self-concern.

*

After his realization in the forest, Gautama, filled with compassion for all things and inspired by the challenge of what he felt he needed to discover, presumably then contemplated how he should set about the search.

He is then said to have had a "vision"—of a religious mendicant (a beggar priest). Gautama asked the "vision" who he was and the mendicant replied that he was a recluse who, terrified by the transitory nature of all things in the world, had decided to lead a homeless life. "Since all that lives is doomed to extinction, I search for salvation from this world and for that most blessed state in which extinction is unknown. Kinsmen and strangers are the same to me, and greed and hate for all this world of sense are the same to me. Wherever I may be, that is my home—the root of a tree, a deserted sanctuary, a hill, a wood. Possessions have I none, no expectations either. Intent on the supreme goal I wander about, accepting any alms I may receive."

This "vision" served as an instruction for Gautama and he knew that he had seen the next step that he had to take.

*

Again, may we find any parallel with our own experience in this?

Once we have "awakened" in our lives to a new and important enthusiasm or realization, we are prepared to abandon much that had previously seemed important to us. For example, when we fall in love, we are moved to sacrifice all other pursuits in response to the overwhelming magic of the emotion and the irresistible attraction of the loved one.

But of course here we are speaking of fundamental questions in life and our parallel will be more in the realm of awakening to the challenges of religion and philosophy; and in *this* context we *all* set out into adult life as "religious mendicants".

Once we have admitted to ourselves that all things, including ourselves, are born, grow old, decay and die—and who can uphold that it is otherwise—then we delude ourselves if we believe that *anything* is other than transitory.

No home is permanent.

No relationship is permanent.

And, as far as our journey through life is concerned, "kinsmen and strangers" are of equal value.

In the final analysis, we are each of us born alone and we will each of us die alone; and all those people we meet during the life in between are at the same time *both* kinsmen *and* strangers. Every single one is a human being and our estimation of each one rises and falls, as time passes and they mean more or less to us according to the harmony or discord of the relationship. And, at the very best, "permanence" of relationship is measured in tens of years.

In the light of this perspective, what sense is there in suffering hatred and indulging greed?

We come into existence in the world and, no matter how we may think of "home" for the purposes of security and sense of permanence, in reality the world is our "temporary home" wherever it may happen to be. "Home" in this sense is not a synonym of "house"; "home" is anywhere we can find to *rest*, physically and mentally, between our continual comings and goings; "home" is the ever-present *centre* that is anywhere and everywhere.

From time to time we have what we call "possessions". But in what permanent sense may we keep any such possessions? Realistically we may say that we have temporary care of certain things. But is it not a delusion to believe that we have any single thing that cannot be taken away from us—or that we will not leave "behind" at our death?

We are led by expectation. Fair enough. We could not do anything if we had no motive or goal. But suffering and delusion lie in what we expect to gain for ourselves from our efforts. *Suffering* comes from the falling short of our imagined expectations . . . disappointment, failure, compromise, being let down, cheated, deprived, deceived . . . all the blame for shortcomings imposed on ourselves and others. *Delusion* lies in the imagined benefits of success. Even if we do manage to attain the fulfilment of expectations, may we ever *rest* in the happiness and glory of worldly achievement? Thus, the point is not that we should refrain from the attempt to achieve and do our best in the attempt, but that we deceive ourselves and suffer through expectation of what benefit the result will bring.

*

85

Paradoxical though it may seem: There is a path to walk on, there is walking being done, but there is no traveller . . .

*

Finally, if we wish to know Truth—and that is the supreme goal for us—and if we also have the humility to accept that *everything* in this life is given to us (for we enter existence or *samsara* with nothing—body, mind, the world and all things in it are "given" to us) . . . then we are truly "religious mendicants"—whether or not we wander from place to place, dressed in saffron robes and carrying a begging bowl.

*

Now, in contrast to the childhood sense of security and permanence, the above commentary may well strike hard and cold. We may at first fear it and shy away from its apparent ruthlessness.

But, if we are prepared to observe and admit . . . is it not the reality of our situation?

And we will surely find that, as we gradually become accustomed to it, unexpectedly it proves to be a considerable step towards liberation. For it has the power to free us of so much; vague theory, glib explanation, useless debate, confused and wishful thinking, deluding and debilitating self-concern.

Gautama found that admitting the realistic view undermines the temptation to indulge in self-pity and clears the mind.

And, in place of the cold and harsh threat to our security, through such realization the heart is touched and may release a cool compassion for all around us.

This, in turn, as understanding develops, leads to the persuasive warmth of selfless love.

*

A kind man who makes good use of wealth is rightly said to possess a great treasure; but the miser who hoards up his riches will have no

86

profit. Charity is rich in return; charity is the greatest wealth, for though it scatters, it brings no repentence . . .

(Sayings of Buddha)

*

After the episode in the forest, Gautama leaves the palace and turns his back on his "former life".

Now perhaps we may begin to sense something more immediate than the vague concept of "past lives" or reincarnation through "open-ended" historical time.

Former . . . a previous or recent form of . . . ever-changing form . . . never permanent . . . a passing form of life . . .

Life . . . ever-present . . . is not born, does not die . . . gives life to form . . . but has no form itself, is not form . . . life does not "belong" to form . . . not "my" life—but life in "me" . . .

Former lives . . . life in changing forms . . . "my" changing form . . . "your" changing form . . . the form of life changes . . .

"Past" and "future" forms . . . but life itself always present . . .

There is no life in past and future forms . . .

"You" and "I" are present forms of life.

Are we then the life or the form . . . or both, conjoined in the present moment?

If I am the form, then I was born and I will die.

If I am both the life and the form, then I will continue for ever, being born and dying, being born and dying . . .

If I am the life itself, then I am never born and will never die.

It all depends on whether I believe . . . which means to give life to form . . . and what I believe . . . which means to become the form.

*

If a caterpillar believes itself to be a caterpillar, then the caterpillar will "die" when it becomes a chrysalis; and if the chrysalis believes itself to be a chrysalis, then the chrysalis will "die" when it becomes a butterfly.

87

Life itself is in the changing form caterpillar-chrysalis-butterfly.

For Gautama the form of life changed.

The purpose of his life re-formed him.

And he did not grieve the passing of his former self, his "former lives".

*

Chandaka, Gautama's charioteer, he who carried Gautama away from the palace in the night and brought him to a hermitage along the road, tried to dissuade Gautama from renouncing his former life.

But Gautama assures him that all things must one day go their separate ways:

". . . Birds settle on a tree for a while, and then go their separate ways again. The meeting of all living beings must likewise inevitably end in their parting. Clouds meet and then fly apart again, and in the same light I see the union of living beings and their parting. This world passes away, and disappoints all hopes of everlasting attachment. It is therefore unwise to have a sense of ownership for people who are united with us in a dream—for a short while only, and not in fact . . ."

So we, like Gautama, part company with what we once were. We do not grieve for our former state once we are on the road to Truth. Do you grieve the loss of the baby-body you once inhabited? No. We are simply grateful to that "charioteer" who has brought us to where we are *now*.

Now . . . the "hermitage" . . . where alone we contemplate the way ahead.

And before Chandaka finally leaves, Gautama says to him:

"Tell them not to feel affection for me but to hear my resolve: 'That either he will find the deathless state and then you will quickly see him again; or he will go to perdition, because his strength has failed and he could not achieve his purpose.'"

*

And so Gautama began his search for that which is not subject to birth, change, ageing and death . . . for the unborn, changeless, ageless and deathless.

Clearly no such "thing" existed in the world of form as he had hitherto experienced and understood it. Although he knew he had to find "the most blessed state in which extinction is unknown", he did not know how to set about finding it.

Accounts differ as to what exactly happened at this juncture but it is generally acknowledged that Gautama undertook a religious and philosophical training and it is recorded that he had two teachers—Kalama and Ramaputta.

It is assumed that he would have been taught in the Vedic tradition—that ancient philosophy from which, as we have already mentioned, derived all that we understand today by the term "Hinduism".

*

And in our case?

What might our fate be as we turn to look for the answers to our deepest questions and aspire to leading a worthwhile and fulfilling life?

We also will probably begin the search by looking for the source of knowledge and wisdom. Our teachers—whether in the flesh or recorded in books—will come in many different forms for their wisdom will have been distilled from widely differing fields of experience and learning. Whatever terminology they happen to use —this or that religion, this or that sect, this or that system or tradition of philosophy, this or that school of psychology, this or that field of science, this or that artistic culture—we will find many teachers who will tell us the truth as to "how it is" and what needs to be done.

Of all the possible fields of endeavour and their disciplines, our own particular nature and circumstances will influence which particular ones we will follow. The likelihood is that we will have very limited options at first and we will be persuaded and imposed upon.

There will be little we can do about this because our knowledge and power of discrimination is not sufficiently developed. We are most likely to be placed under the influence of our family's religion—if they subscribe to one; and, in addition to those subjects which are compulsory, in our education we shall find ourselves being taught by the teachers of those disciplines for which we seem to have an aptitude or which are deemed necessary for taking a place in our particular society and pursuing a "chosen" career.

If we ignore the doctrine of *karma*, it seems a matter of chance and luck whether we are appropriately and sensibly taught and whether we come under the influence of wise or foolish teachers.

*

The Teacher sees the universe face to face and understands its nature. He proclaims the truth both in its letter and in its spirit, and his doctrine is glorious in its origin, glorious in its progress, glorious in its consummation. The Teacher reveals the higher life in its purity and perfection . . .

(*Sayings of Buddha*)

*

Gautama's intensive religious and philosophical training must have appealed to him and confirmed him in the role and method of the "religious mendicant" for the next celebrated episode finds him committed to the ascetic life of a wandering "monk". He has taken vows and renounced pleasures and pursuits of the world and is practising austere disciplines of self-denial. And, in seeking a secluded and peaceful retreat for the purpose of carrying out the disciplines and contemplation, he joins five other mendicants on the bank of a river. It is said that they "waited upon him in their desire for liberation . . . bowed before him, followed his instructions, and placed themselves as pupils under his control, just as the restless senses serve the mind."

*

As we explore the various possibilities open to us in life, we choose those courses that seem to offer the most promise of satisfying our desires.

This process runs through all our activity, from the most mundane and trivial to the most important. Whether it is choosing what to eat for breakfast, choosing an entertainment, choosing what clothes to buy, choosing what subjects to study, choosing what book to read, choosing what religious practice to undertake, all of them are directed towards satisfying what we think we lack. Once we have made a choice, our five senses, awaiting the summons, are directed by will to taking in the relevant experience.

Whatever it is that we believe will contribute to our happiness and contentment ("liberate our desires"), we will withdraw our attention from that which is irrelevant. Less and less are we able to indulge in vague and idle dreams as we concentrate on pursuit of that which will fulfil our growing expectations.

Among the wealth of possibilities, very few of us will be minded or able to follow Gautama's example literally and subordinate all pursuits to the religious and philosophical quest. Even if we do rate them very highly, it is not easy to give them top priority in a twentieth-century world with its emphasis on material wealth, food, entertainment, competition, science, technology, and so on.

But even if only a few of us can become "professional" religious officials or academic philosophers, we may still become intensely religious or philosophical in our outlook on life and its activities.

Once we are convinced of the over-riding importance of finding "the road to salvation"—the most noble of man's aspirations with its connotations of service to others and obedience to the "natural law"—we are then mentally prepared to subordinate all other concerns and impose on ourselves all manner of self-denial, according to the dictates of what we have understood from our teachers and their interpretations of their traditions.

*

Each of us will start from where he is *now*.

My "cup is full"; your "cup is full"; (of what? self-concern?)
The *dharma* flows like a stream of tea from the divine pot.
"Drop by drop the vessel is filled."
But if the cup is full the tea will overflow and stream away.

It may seem like suicide at first, to give up all our ideas and our opinions and beliefs.

The self-denial may not be "sackcloth and ashes" but the "giving up" or "letting go" of all our accumulation of habitual thinking and believing, reacting and behaving.

We may say: "But what about *me*?"

But how else may "I" be filled?

*

"*How can I show you Zen unless you first empty your cup?*"

Six

Tanzan and Ekido were once travelling together down a muddy road. A heavy rain was still falling.

Coming round a bend they met a lovely girl in a silk kimono and sash, unable to cross the intersection.

"Come on, girl," said Tanzan at once. Lifting her in his arms, he carried her over the mud.

Ekido did not speak until that night when they reached a lodging temple. Then he could no longer restrain himself. "We monks don't go near females," he told Tanzan, "especially not young and lovely ones. It is dangerous. Why did you do that?"

"I left the girl there," said Tanzan. "Are you still carrying her?"

Zen story

*

The next stage in Gautama's story is easy to relate—but may be far from easy for us to respond to from our own personal experience.

To put it quite simply, after spending six years in the ascetic life, Gautama realized that the course he was following was not going to provide for him the answer to his search for "the deathless state".

Psychologically we may perhaps imagine just how critical an admission this must have been. It is never easy after a long period of commitment and even sacrifice to admit that you have been "wrong".

Wrong? We may see in retrospect that it is never "wrong" in the sense of utterly wasted. Whatever course of action we have taken it is through that course that we arrive at our new point. It

93

took Gautama six years to reach the conclusion that the ascetic life —and it is said that his fasting and self-denial was so rigorous that . . . "His fat, flesh and blood had all gone. Only skin and bone remained"—was not leading him to his ultimate goal, "the further, the unbounded shore, of Samsara". However, we may see that, in order to come to that conclusion, he had first to go through the disillusionment of the former course of action. This in itself may give us a great clue to so many of the Buddhist doctrinal concepts. *Karma* for instance is perfectly reflected here.

The *former life* was not "wrong"—and therefore in the *present life* you are as it were "paying the penalty". The former life is simply the opportunity for the present life. You could not be what you are now without having been what you were then. What you are *now* is Buddha-potential; what you were *then* was Buddha-potential. There is no *now* and *then*, there is only Buddha. *Now* and *then* is illusion. But it is only by passing through illusion that we may come to know illusion and it is only by coming to know illusion that we may give it up!

The same could equally be said of "suffering"; until you have suffered you cannot know suffering and until you know suffering you cannot give up your suffering. But, it could be argued, before you suffered there was no suffering to give up! Why go into the suffering in the first place?

Why indeed!

Here again, the Gautama story may come to our aid.

Before Gautama left the palace and saw the suffering in the world outside, he was free of suffering—but ignorant of *samsara*. In other words he did not know that he was bound, having been born, to grow old and die. Once he went outside the protective shell of the palace he began to suffer—but through his suffering he resolved to find "the deathless state".

Thus the suffering, which we would deem to be "wrong", was the vital impulse that set Gautama on his journey to Buddha-hood.

And now we have come to the second vital moment—the giving up of the ascetic life.

Such moments could be referred to as "intervals".

In its usual usage an "interval" means a pause or an intervening time or space; however, here we are using the word in its musical connotation. In music an interval is the difference of frequency between two sounds, in melody or harmony. Thus the sound (or "note") *before* the interval calls for the sound *after* the interval for the melody or harmony to be; and similarly the sound *after* the interval requires the sound *before* the interval to place it and give it its particular form. In other words the *new* sound's frequency could not be built without its predecessors (any more than a man could be "born" at 30 years of age but requires the baby, child, adolescent, adult scale . . .) and the *old* sound is not realized, fulfilling the potential of the melody, without the emergence of its "heir"—the immediately related higher note (any more than a baby could be said to have been fulfilled if it is "born" dead).

It may seem paradoxical to start using a musical vernacular within this book, but anyone who has read *The Hindu Sound* will already have been introduced to the idea of a direct parallel between the musical progression through the scale or octave with the subtle (mental), spiritual path to awakening.

And so, in Gautama's life, there are certain crucial moments when his whole being is about to be changed in pitch and quality by reaching a point of realization, and these moments are directly similar to (what we are calling) major "intervals".

*

In lesser ways, in our own experience, we may well recognize such intervals.

From early in our childhood we will each of us know what it means to realize that a certain course of action is not going to bring about the desired result.

It all depends on the *desire*.

Gautama had a *single-minded* desire for "the deathless state".

It will be very rare, if ever, that you or I will experience an absolutely single-minded desire—to the complete exclusion of everything else—but if I want something enough, I will certainly direct attention to the means of getting it. This can be on the scale of trivial, daily desires such as wanting a certain thing to eat or to be entertained in a certain way; or it can be on the scale of longer term goals, weeks, months or even years ahead. No matter what the scale, no sooner have I started on a particular course of action to achieve my desired result, then I will continually monitor the effects of my actions in relation to the goal I have set myself. In the lesser, more trivial areas I will very often achieve my goals—and then I move on to my next pursuit. (Where again, at the juncture of having attained an objective, there will be an "interval". I have to consider what to do next. Again this may be on the scale of the completion of a small, daily task or the completion of a phase of life which may have taken years to accomplish.) With the large scale, longer term goals—such as reaching the peaks of a chosen career or successfully establishing a home and family—the imagined results are vaguer and more difficult to assess and things can easily go awry. It is in these pursuits particularly that I may well come across the "intervals" that we spoke of above.

What happens then?

The strength of my desire will dictate my next step.

In what we might call materialistic aims, I may well give up the pursuit if it does not seem worthwhile making further effort—and thus compromise myself and divert my attention to something else.

In other words I *evaluate*.

I evaluate or weigh the required effort against the anticipated value of the result. So I may give it up or, if I think it worth the effort, I will direct my attention with determination in getting across the interval (the unexpected break in progress) and try to overcome or by-pass the obstacle.

This is the moment of decision.

Is it worth it?

Shall I continue to expend energy and time on this pursuit?

Or again, if I have completed one task, is it worth pursuing the next one?

As we have said, in the small, daily concerns, it will not matter too much. If I cannot have, say, the apple that I want or am not able to watch the television programme that I like, then I will notice the *disappointment* (a depressing, dull or sharp, discomfort in mind) but I soon recover and move on to something else.

But as the scale of the desire or goal increases, the effort required will be greater and, the higher I evaluate the desired result, the more I expose myself to the pain of greater disappointment.

In the realm of materialistic aims, although I may concentrate for years on the ways and means to acquire certain possessions—and may become neurotic, angered, embittered, ruthless, insensitive and all sorts of other things in the process—I may still not be deterred. And, despite the "ill-state" I may drive myself, *and others*, into, if the desire has become obsessive, I will not give up—until I finally drop dead. Of course this is far more serious. My fear of failure and disappointment becomes so great that I do not see or I ignore the opportunity for re-assessment offered by the intervals caused by periodic obstacles and set-backs. In short, I do not *evaluate*.

Gautama, faced with the growing or sudden realization that the rigorous ascetic life he was living with the five mendicants was not going to lead him to his *one* and *only* desire—"the deathless state"—simply gave up the ascetic life; no two ways about it; he turned his back on six years of tortuous endeavour. He *evaluated* the situation and acted on his evaluation.

Gautama was set on the path to Buddha-hood—and it surely cannot be coincidence that the Sanskrit word of the organ of mind which evaluates is called *buddhi*.

*

Though a person be ornamented with jewels, the heart may have conquered the senses. The outward form does not constitute religion or affect the mind. Thus the body of a hermit may wear an ascetic's garb while his mind is immersed in worldliness. A man who dwells in lonely woods and yet covets worldly vanities, is a worldling, while the man in worldly garments may let his heart soar high to heavenly thoughts. There is no distinction between the layman and the hermit, if both have banished the thought of self.

(*Sayings of Buddha*)

*

Of course, particularly in Western culture, determination is often seen as a virtue in itself. Very often our "successful" men and women are characterized by their extraordinary application to the achievement of their particular goal.

But let us look at the historical evidence.

What were the motives of such "heroes" and "heroines"?

At what cost did they achieve?

Were they self-obsessed or altruistic?

To what extent did they really understand *man's* purpose in life —tied as they were to their own particular goal.

It is dangerous to theorise—and of course none of us can speak for anyone else—but perhaps we may quote a maxim (which may be of Buddhist derivation):

"Man thinks he ought to be a success; woman thinks she will be a failure."

Success and *failure* both so intricately linked—just as the *male* and *female* elements are so precisely and precariously balanced within each of us.

If the "male" in me thinks I ought to be a success—then the "female" in me will immediately be alerted to being a failure.

But on such occasions we must ask ourselves the question:

"In relation to what goal may I truly be judged a success or failure?"

Determination may be a virtue—but we have to be very sure in relation to what goal and we should not be too easily influenced by the world's estimation of success and failure. Such estimations may well prove to be a short-cut to the "ill-state". People only lack determination because they have not yet found that which is truly worth pursuing.

98

Was Gautama a *success*—in that he achieved Buddha-hood?

Or was he a *failure* as a mendicant?

Both questions are clearly absurd—but can we see the same absurdity in our assessment of our own state?

*

This same pattern indeed applies in what we might call the aesthetic or non-materialistic aims.

Here the problem becomes more subtle because such pursuits are likely to be considered more "laudable" and "noble" in the eyes of the world and the worth of the goal is less easy to assess.

It may be my desire to be the "best" of priests, doctors, mothers, lawyers, musicians, scientists, actors, politicians, authors, journalists, diplomats, social workers or whatever. Many such pursuits may be engaged in for "higher" aims than simply material gain.

It may be argued that almost any occupation could be regarded as contributing to "social need" and need never be entirely material-istic. But that is up to the individual "conscience" and "social need"—and materialistic plenty is not the level of motivation we are reaching for here. It is a much more elusive aspiration than that; perhaps we could call it "man's search for truth and happiness".

This "aesthetic" level of aim involves lifetime commitment, in the sense that such occupations require years of training and experience, and "success" in whatever field may well not be achieved until we are well advanced in life.

The trouble is that we are likely to commit ourselves to such occupation on the slenderest, most facile, haphazard and, above all, the vaguest of motives. The influences which lead to the decision to *become* a priest, doctor, lawyer, actor, etc., are many and varied— but we are committed to the occupation *before* we have the power to reason *why* we want to do it and *before* we have had any actual experience of doing it!

One of the most familiar questions of all our early adolescent lives must be:

"What are you going to be when you grow up?"

99

Note that "be"!

It would be pretty hard to answer with certainty: "What are you going to *do* . . .?" But: "What are you going to *be* . . .?"

The sort of answers one would love to give are: "Alive", or "happy" . . . "enlightened" . . . "Buddha" . . .

And it is common enough to observe that in commitment to the training and then experience of the practice of our chosen career, we tend to ignore and fail to contemplate along the way *why* we are doing it. And the further committed and the further along the way we are, the harder it is for us to admit that we may be doing the wrong thing . . . and so we may just settle for living out our lives with suppressed dissatisfaction. And in time the dissatisfaction may become so much a part of our view of the world that it becomes an end in itself—just as a crutch becomes a substitute for a leg to walk on—and we find it difficult to even contemplate doing without it.

Strangely enough, one of the hardest things to give up is our suffering. Usually we have to wait for it to "go away".

Have you ever been in love, and not been loved in return? The pain of not attaining your desire is almost unbearable—there is only one thing harder, and that is giving up the pain! For in giving up the *pain* we are giving up also our *desire*—and we "cannot live", we say, "without that desire".

*

We should perhaps pause here and consider another aspect of man's ability to experience as an individual and separate human being.

Because we believe that we are each of us a particular body with a particular shape, with particular features and a particular name, we also believe that our experiences are peculiar to each of us. Indeed we have kept on repeating in this book and the others of this series that no one else can experience for us. Now this is clearly so. If I have a pain—only I can "feel" that pain; you cannot feel it for me, you cannot take it from me and suffer it in my stead. The pain is caused by something having happened to *my body*, which is being registered in *my mind*. The most that you can do is try to alleviate the cause of the pain in my body. Thus, if you are a doctor, say, you will attempt to cure the ill, and if you are a loving friend you will support me and look after my needs in the hope that the pain will soon pass. The one thing that neither the doctor nor the friend can do is have the pain for me.

However, human beings have another extraordinary capacity; they can "sympathize".

Sympathy is defined in the dictionary as: "Community of feeling: Power of entering into another's feelings or mind: Harmonious understanding: Compassion, pity: Affinity or correlation whereby one thing responds to the action of another or to action upon another ..."

From very early in life, perhaps from the very first moment of our entry into the samsaric world, each of us will begin to experience events peculiar to our karma and the way we experience the events will also be particular to our own karmic disposition. And so, indeed, we will seem to be entirely separated from one another.

Where then is the link with one another? Where is any understanding to come from? How will we ever communicate; how will we ever understand one another?

What is *sympathy*, this "power of entering into another's feelings or mind"? Where does it spring from? What is its cause?

Sympathy is an *emotion*, perhaps the highest of the *emotions*, and it is through the emotions that human understanding and communion comes about.

The love that one person feels for another is beyond *reason*; we cannot intellectualize why we love each other; we may try; we may say that two people are compatible, that they share common interests; we may even say that "opposites attract"; we may find all manner of reasons why people "love"—and an equal number for why people "hate"—but none of the reasons will explain the mysterious surge of sympathy, the strange alchemy, that is experienced at given moments between friends, loved ones, and sometimes even strangers that one meets briefly in a crowd or on a lonely road.

The working of emotion "through the heart" is beyond the reasoning of mind and yet it is essential to mind in its role of interpreter and we may come to see that when the mind eventually is disciplined and ceases its constant battle to "work things out" that the emotions (and by this we mean the purest and highest emotions) make a connection in which there is no explanation needed for there is simply Knowledge.

*

What Knowledge?

Of ONENESS

That the "I" in you and the "I" in me is the same "I".

In pure emotion ("flowing out from") the "you" and the "me" may "flow into" each other.

Again we may question whether these "emotions" are not peculiar to each individual being. After all we do not all suffer the same tragedies, we are not all blessed with the same fortunes. It is not the *form* of suffering that matters; it is the suffering itself.

It is highly unlikely that you or I will dedicate ourselves so rigorously to a discipline that—like Gautama—we will be reduced to "mere skin and bone".

It is here that sympathy plays such an important part.

A mother may find her baby dead in its cot one morning, a young child may find her kitten dead . . . the two events are poles apart as "tragedies" in worldly terms—but the anguish to the child and the anguish to the mother stem from the same root, the loss is overwhelming, the sorrow possesses them equally.

If I have toothache and the pain is acute, will it help me one iota to be told that there are worse pains? But if you tell me that you are in pain, and that the pain is almost unbearable—can I not sympathize? For I also have experienced pain; not the same pain, not your pain—but *pain*, detached, neutral—a condition experienced in *mind*.

Now this may seem extremely harsh but if the baby is dead what use is the mother's anguish? Will it bring the baby back to life; will it in any way alter the event . . . an event which is already in the past? If the kitten is dead, will the child's anguish revive the kitten?

If the pain is physical—as with the toothache—then obviously I will seek to get rid of it. If the pain is mental—in the mind—as with the anguish of the mother, then why hang on to it? Why not let it go also? If I am in sympathy with you, then I will gladly take it from you, and share it.

*

Gautama suffered the rigours of the mendicant's life for six years, and it may well be that you or I, viewing the events as uninvolved outsiders, may wonder why he put up with it for so long. But, rather than concerning ourselves with another person's story, we might be better advised, once again to look to our own.

Gautama's story must surely stand as an example to each and every one of us. It is not that we should copy his life in its every detail—that would never be possible—but rather that through the example of his life we should look at our own experiences anew.

Gautama believed that with the mendicants he would find the way to the deathless state. So strong was his belief, so dedicated his desire, that he put himself literally "body and soul" into the discipline. It is said that at meal-times he ate but a single grain of rice, so intent was he "upon winning the further, the unbounded shore of *samsara*".

But eventually it became clear to him that this supreme self-torture was merely wearing away the body to no useful purpose.

How one may sympathize with him (although none of us will have had an entirely similar experience) in this moment of crushing disillusionment. All that he had been working for—and working with such single-minded dedication—suddenly appeared to him as far away as ever; his method was in error.

He is said to have reasoned something like this:

"This is not the *Dharma* which leads to dispassion, to enlighten-ment, to emancipation . . .

"When the body is worn down and exhausted by hunger and thirst, the mind in its turn must feel the strain, that mental organ that must reap the fruit . . .

"Inward calm is needed for success! . . .

"Only if the body is reasonably nourished can undue strain on the mind be avoided. When the mind is free from strain and is serene, than the faculty of Transic concentration can arise in it. When thought is joined to Transic concentration, then it can advance through the various stages of trance. We can then win the *dharma* which finally allows us to gain the highest state, so hard to reach, which is tranquil, ageless and deathless. And without proper nourishment this procedure is quite impossible . . ."

*

The disillusionment for him of the mendicant's way was complete.

We also, in our own lives, will experience moments when all our efforts seem to have been in vain. We may have been working towards some desired goal, be it success in our work, in the fulfilment of a dream, in the acquiring of some special object, in the winning of respect or the love of some other person. In all such cases we have committed ourselves to a particular aim.

And it is here that we come to the possibility of a major interval.

For once we have set out along the path to whatever goal we believed desirable, we may find disillusionment awaiting us along the way.

What is this course leading to?

Have I done the wrong thing?

Disillusionment is imminent; the realization that it is not leading me where I wanted to go and, yes, I have done the wrong thing.

This may happen earlier or later, in varying degrees of intensity.

(Or perhaps not at all, if we are undeterred right through to death and never falter in confidence. Such a situation is not our concern here. We might say that he is either a lucky man or an ignorant one who can maintain such confidence to the point of death—if, indeed, there could be such a man.)

But disillusionment—if it comes—is an interval and a challenge indeed.

In some contexts, we may simply be able to change course and pursue something else. But what we are talking about here—if we can pitch it as high as possible, to the kind of level represented by Gautama—is a profound psychological crisis. For here we are speaking about disillusionment which shatters a lifetime's conditioning (and, as we have said it may seem sudden or gradual).

For some it may penetrate to "the depths of the soul".

It is not just a case of disillusionment with something as serious as realizing that years of pursuit in say a career or marriage, have been pointless and wasted; that can be remedied within the world's possibilities and in any case is only the symptom of the problem— *the mind's illusion.*

We have believed ourselves to be "something", to be going "somewhere"—and now we are disillusioned.

Disillusion really only exists in the realms of belief.

It can, for example, mean the realization that everything that one has believed in is suspect. It may be a "waking up" to the knowledge that all the dreams that the mind has conjured up, entertained, adopted and trusted are seen to be unrealizable. It may be the realization that *all* that one has trusted is insubstantial make-believe and not an absolute and undeniable truth that can be relied upon.

*

The mind's reaction to disillusionment of this calibre can be very varied. It may be one of shock, fear, despair, desperation. There will be suffering. Anguish. Agony.

Disillusion causes mental disturbance and, in extreme cases, the mind may cease to function "normally" and refuse to continue to cope with life. In the less extreme cases the person concerned may have recourse to "escape" methods; for example, drugs and pain-killers in various forms, whether officially approved of or otherwise.

For such reasons, disillusion (couched in many different terms) is commonly regarded as negative. And the usual response and exhortation comes in such forms as "forget it," "pull yourself together," "get on with it," "you'll get over it," and so on.

But, when you come to consider it, is this not rather strange?

"Get over" what?

The disillusion?

Should not dis-illusion be a positive event?

Can it be sensible to live in illusion?

Surely it should be a *relief* to be freed from illusion?

Could it not be that such re-lief is freedom from be-lief?

Why should we pursue illusion and fear disillusion?

Unless perhaps it is because our supposed security will be threatened.

Ultimately what security is there in illusion?

Perhaps the disturbance which accompanies disillusion might be due to the *mind* not having been *prepared to tell the truth*?

Is not the Truth what we are seeking?

And if Truth is our single-minded desire then should we not welcome all dis-illusionment?

If we are to understand and follow Gautama's example and teaching we should be prepared . . . to realize that "the Way" is one of continuing disillusion.

In his terms the mind is "covered" with five *skandhas* or sheaths of illusion (*maya*) and our *development* is a matter of *removing illusion rather than pursuing Truth*.

Thus the aesthetic and the mendicant may say "I am not here to be happy" but The Enlightened One will say "There is no reason for unhappiness".

When the illusion is removed, Truth is dis-covered as self-evident.

*

By the banks of the river we may guess at and sympathize with the supreme disillusion of Gautama. He had committed himself to the wisdom and tradition of his ancestors. This, as he now understood it, was not relevant to what he wished to discover.

106

He was prepared to renounce it.

The disillusion did not defeat him. A lesser man might have gone back to the palace and resumed his position of worldly privilege; a lesser man might have gone on with the disciplines unto death.

But not Gautama.

*

We may indeed feel that six years was a long time to spend before realizing something that we today would probably consider common sense. But we should perhaps reflect how long it might take us to be prepared to renounce "the vision and beliefs of our fathers", especially if they are of a religious nature and we have made solemn vows of obedience.

And let us also continue to consider the event in parallel with our own experience and not just at the literal, mundane level.

Sympathy does not compare; sympathy never condemns.

Sympathy understands through recognition and communicates through silent listening.

If we are sympathetic to Gautama's moment of disillusionment we do not pity him with mawkish and sentimental dreams of how it should have been for him. Rather may we silently acknowledge the reflection of his example in our own captive state.

If we live in the wealthier of the world's societies our bodies may be adequately fed at all times and thus our minds may be keen and active.

But what about the "mental food" on which we feed our minds?

We fill our minds with a wealth of impressions and work them to learn about and pursue all manner of occupation. This in turn gives rise to continual thinking, evaluating, imagining, dreaming, striving for solutions, and so on. This is a continual strain on the mind, creating tensions, worries, anxieties, fears.

How serene are you?

How serene am I?

How intelligently do we seek the kind of mental food which will restore the spirit, inspire and guide us towards a lasting happiness and realization of our purpose?

In our pre-occupation with physical survival and sensual appetite, may we not be guilty of starving the mind into a state of spiritual exhaustion?

We tend to become influenced by what we have learned and believed to be of value in the world's terms that we leave little time or space to listen to our own intuition and to allow our own intelligence to contemplate the mysteries of life. By this we do not mean absorbing and analysing more and more of *other people's* interpretations of the mysteries, even although they may help us from time to time; it means our own understanding of them, based on observation of our own experience.

It cannot be emphasized enough that learning about other people's realizations is absolutely no substitute for realizing in one's own way for oneself. It is about as different as seeing a photograph rather than being at the actual place. However, if we take the analogy a little further, if you have already been to the place, such a photograph may evoke recognition ("re-knowing") and memory of what it is like to be there. Thus the record of other people's experiences can be valuable if it reminds us of our own experience and helps to confirm our own realizations.

So it is that we may find reassurance, strength and confirmation in Gautama's story—as we find our own story reflected in it.

*

Buddha said:
Be ye lamps unto yourselves,
Be ye your own reliance.
Hold to the truth within yourselves,
As to the only lamp.

*

And so Gautama goes down the river bank to bathe—as if to wash away his "former life". But also as if to prepare himself for the new life ahead.

There he encounters Nandabala, "daughter of the chief cowherd" who is honoured and overjoyed to be able to provide him with his first sustaining food, so that he may begin to regain his strength.

How like a new birth it seems; like an absolution, like a beginning.

The past is behind him, he does not "carry it with him". He is naked, unprotected, empty. Ahead lies a total unknown. All that carries him forward is his unique spirit, freed from illusion . . . waiting.

So might our minds, dulled and exhausted by a diet lacking nourishment, be delighted that we have made the decision to "eat proper food again".

Of course his five companions, the religious mendicants, disapprove of his abandoning his vows and disciplines; it is natural that they should do so. Is he not, after all, a threat to their own security, a threat to their beliefs? And so they leave him.

Gautama knows he is alone in the world.

So might we meet disapproval when we decide to spurn the vows and discipline that our worldly teachers approve of—not only from those teachers themselves but also from that conditioned part of the mind which still wishes to cling to learning and belief.

So be it:

"Be ye lamps unto yourselves . . ."

*

Gautama is undeterred. Such is the calibre of his nature he has the courage and is prepared to sacrifice everything. His determination to discover the Truth will not be gainsaid.

But what can he do?

He now has no other person nor worldly wisdom to turn to.

"Accompanied only by his resolution, he proceeded to the root of a sacred fig-tree, where the ground was carpeted with green grass. For he was definitely determined to win full enlightenment soon."

It is as if his determination communicates itself to a "higher" faculty of his mind—or even beyond his mind—to a kind of certain knowledge which we might call "intuition" or "conscience", a feature which we do not commonly evoke and listen to. This is represented by Kala, "a serpent of high rank", who says:

"Your steps, O Sage, resound like thunder reverberating in the earth; the light that issues from your body shines like the sun: No doubt that you today will taste the fruit you so desire! The flocks of blue jays which are whirling round up in the sky show their respect by keeping their right sides towards you; the air is full of gentle breezes: It is quite certain that today you will become a Buddha."

*

Gautama collects grass from a grass cutter and sits down in a cross-legged posture beneath the tree.

He vows that he will not change his position under the tree until he has accomplished what he has set out to do.

The beasts and the birds fall silent.

Even the leaves cease to rustle when moved by the wind.

It is as if the world comes to an end . . .

as Gautama meditates . . .

on Truth.

Seven

Think of not thinking of anything at all. How is one to think of not thinking of anything at all? Be without thoughts—this is the secret of meditation.

(From *Zazengi*)

*

Each of our chapters so far has begun with a Zen story. The word "Zen" (in Chinese, *Ch'an*) comes from the Sanskrit word, *Dhyana*. The word *Dhyana* can mean "Meditation".

Each of our stories, enigmatic in its nature, represents an aspect of the essential power of meditation. The depth of the stories cannot be intellectually appreciated. If we rely upon intellect to interpret them then they may well seem trite, shallow, unimportant, even silly. They are stories without ends; what happens to the man, after he has eaten the wild strawberry? Presumably he falls to his death! When the listener dies, why doesn't the harpist find another listener? Why cut the strings and play no more? Is this not a denial of his gift? Where does a snowflake go to, dissolving in the pure air? Can trees and grass become enlightened? Is that what it means? If I wanted to discuss something as important and as deep as meditation —would I not be dismayed if my master merely spilt a cup of tea? And as for the monk who broke his vows and carried the girl across the road . . . how can he excuse himself? There is no excuse!

These reactions may be rather trite in themselves and there may be readers who are saying "Oh, no—I get the point of such and such a story . . . It means so-and-so . . ."

But does it?

"Yes, it does!" the reader will answer.

To whom?

"To *me*!" the reader will reply.

To me.

As an experience can only be what it is for you and cannot be directly shared—so meaning is equally exclusive. We may indicate *a* meaning to each other, but, ultimately, meaning is in your mind and meaning is in my mind. Could there, therefore, be *two* meanings both quite different—one of them "yours" and one of them "mine"? Or is there *no* meaning, but simply how each of us responds to it in mind?

And if my mind does not make a meaning, then is the story "meaningless"?

Or is it, perhaps, "beyond me" as we say—implying that it is too clever for me to understand.

Then again—how do we *understand*?

Do we not understand through recognizing what we already know in our own experience?

When we "understand something for the first time"—what has happened? Either a process of preparation has gone on in mind which brings us to our moment of understanding. (Thus, for example, we learn the basic rules, grammar and vocabulary of a language and, through our learning, grow into understanding someone speaking that language.) Or, not nearly so often, quite suddenly we *know* something. (Examples here are more difficult to find and to write about. Have you ever met a friend and as you see him, you know that all is not well with him? Before he even speaks, you know that he is unhappy. Is it the way he looks—or is it an "instinctive" response to some "thing" in him? A recognition...)

In the first example (learning) the process is conducted by the intellect; in the second example (recognition) the response comes through intuition *from* the "heart".

And now we approach the climax of Gautama's story.

"It is quite certain that today," Kala tells him, "you will become a Buddha."

And how will this be accomplished?
Through meditation.

*

What is meditation?
You can learn all *about it* in innumerable books; all that is said *about it*, all the claims made *about it* by all the innumerable practitioners; all the methods of meditation—and perhaps there are as many methods as there are people who meditate; all the disciplines and all the forms and all the aims of meditation. Intellect can, if it is diligent, learn all there is to learn *about* meditation.

But you will still not *know* meditation . . . until you experience meditating.

What does cabbage taste like? It tastes like cabbage.

How do I know what it tastes like to you? I don't need to; I only need to know what it tastes like to me!

Until I taste cabbage I will *never* know what cabbage tastes like. It is not possible that it should be otherwise.

And when I know what it tastes like I will *never* be able to describe it.

For it is what it is—to me.

It is what it is—to you.

So it is with meditation.

Certainly you may be taught a technique—or a number of techniques.

It is similar to being taught to play a musical instrument. You may be taught, you may practise and you may become a proficient player of that instrument—but the sounds that the instrument *makes* will come *through you*—without you, there would be no sound, and with you, the sound will be peculiarly *yours alone*.

Thus, if you have two master violinists, both playing the same piece of music, the sounds they make will differ as they each differ. Neither sound will be better or worse, they will simply be the individually expressed sounds of each violinist. (You may prefer one sound to the other, but that is a different matter and is to do with your individual reception or listening.)

If you do not *learn* the technique of playing an instrument then the sounds you make may be discordant and malformed (although in some cases, an "infant prodigy" may appear to play an instrument with hardly any tutorage at all). But no one can be *taught* to be a master violinist; no one can be *taught* to be a divine singer, or an inspired artist. The inspiration, the divinity and the master-hood come from within.

Meditation is a little like that, but the analogy is limited. For all the works of man are performances given by man to mankind and our appreciation of the performance will depend upon our particular background, environment, up-bringing and so on. In this way, to the Western ear an African Bushman's chant may seem ugly and discordant while to the Bushman it may be a thing of beauty; to the Western eye certain physical attributes may be considered beautiful, while to the Bushman quite other attributes may be admired and so on (and of course, our "tastes" alter with the passing years and with changing "fashions").

But the taste "cabbage" does not alter! Nor is the taste "cabbage" —if our taste sense is fully developed—ever the same . . . for the conditions will have altered each time we take a mouthful.

Does not alter—and never the same? A contradiction? Or two separate events?

NOW is limitless. NOW is . . . what is NOW.

And so confusion comes in once again as *mind* tries, so diligently, so painstakingly, to understand.

You cannot understand meditation. You can simply meditate.

Be without thoughts—this is the secret of meditation . . .

*

But what is it?

Is it a technique? In that case, you might be better at it than I am?

But better at what? Better in whose estimation?

114

Better at the technique? And the technique is for what? Being without thoughts?

Do you breathe better than I breathe? Or do we both breathe to the best of our abilities?

Do you live better than I live? If you live longer than me is that a better life?

Are you more beautiful than I am? Perhaps you are taller—and "tall", it is decided, "is beautiful"—is your tallness anything to do with you and therefore should I compliment you on having achieved it? And is my shortness something to do with me and therefore have I failed in not being taller?

Of course these arguments are absurd—but strange, isn't it, that we do actually make such judgements?

Let us try a simple definition:

Meditation is to the spirit what breathing is to the body.

*

We *think* we know a lot about the body.

We *think* we know very little, if anything, about the spirit.

Between the body and the spirit there is a vast gulf, and the gulf we call "mind".

We breathe that the body may "live". If we cease to breathe, we are "dead".

Our breathing keeps the heart beating. The heart beating is the symbol of life.

Breath, entering the body, passing through the lungs, oxygenates the blood which in turn passes through the heart and enlivens the body cells . . .

A moment later, we breathe out . . . and then the process starts again.

But we are not just a body.

There is that in us which will respond other than physically.

There is that in us which can "flow out" for the suffering of another person or for mankind; there is that in us which can experience bliss when hearing a blackbird singing at dusk, or a phrase of music, or in the scent of a rose, or in just seeing a loved one's face. At such times, we say, "our spirit is touched."

We do not *think* about breathing—we breathe.

We do not *think* about the scent of a rose—we just smell it.

*

Bound, as we are, within the body, that is born and is sure to die, Gautama sought "the deathless state". Knowing that his *body* must perish he sought the *spirit*. To reach from his *body* to the *spirit* he had to cross the *mind*. To cross over the *mind* he had to still all the activity he found in it.

Once there is no thinking—where is mind?

Once there is no thinking—what separates the body from the spirit?

Once there is no thinking—where is suffering; where is "beginning", where is "ending"?

If mind is still and empty—where is the separation?

If mind is still . . . and empty . . .

*

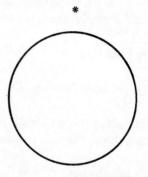

A line with no beginning or ending we call "a circle".

Who first drew a circle and why?

What was conveyed to the man and what did he feel as he drew it?

What do we feel, now, as we look at a circle?

What does it say to us?

We can draw a circle.

What are we trying to convey by doing so?

What are the qualities and nature of a circle?

To concentrate the mind on what the never-beginning and never-ending line means is to contemplate or meditate upon it.

Instead of trying to make it convey something *for* us, we let it "speak" *to* us.

As a symbol, it has the power to order and direct the mind's ability to evaluate and know.

It is man's power of imagination which enables him to understand the nature and laws of the universe through symbols.

Such is the power of imagination that if I am told that the two-dimensional circle above represents a "sphere", then I imagine the third dimension—a hemisphere coming out towards me on this side of the page and another hemisphere receding from me on the other side of the page.

I may even be able to help the imagination with another two-dimensional line.

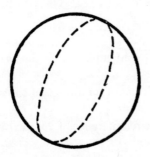

How am I able to do this?

And is this the full limit of my powers?

Supposing the mind's powers can go further, into a realm where time and distance have no relevance, into further dimensions?

And supposing that beyond mind's limits there are other powers available in or through me; unknown, because beyond mind, but waiting to be discovered *through* mind?

Such is the power of meditation . . .

*

A circle (or sphere) . . . a form in space . . . the symbol of total nothing.

Consider it as being alone . . .

To itself, it is neither "large" nor "small" because there is no other with which to compare its size.

To itself, it is neither still nor moving because there is no other in relation to which it can be said to be either not moving or moving.

To itself, it has no "inside" nor "outside" because there is no other, with an independent location, to know which is which.

To itself, here and there are the same, everywhere and nowhere are the same, coming and going and standing still are the same.

There is only "space" in relation to the "being" of the form "circle".

. . . Space . . . . . . and . . . . . . Circle . . . . . . and . . . . . . Space.

*

Let the mind NOW contemplate a single form in space . . . *yourself*.

Become calm and clear of mind . . . self contained . . . a "sphere" of simply *being*.

Reach out to the circumference of your existence.

Where is the limit?

Reach for the centre of yourself.

Where is it?

The universe is alone.

What distance is there between you and the universe?

When the mind ceases to think "I am" in relation to this, that and the other, where am I?

Who am I?

What is the universe?

Am I and the universe separated?

By what?

*

All our experience, all our activity, is appreciated and evaluated in mind and, to ourselves, it seems as though what we think we are is a kind of "interface" between us and the universe.

It is like a thin "surface" of conceiving and thinking which we create so that we seem separate from "the world out there".

And since we think vaguely of ourselves as the centre, we think of ourselves as surrounded by a sphere of experience.

The mind in its working traces patterns on this "spherical surface", etching the designs of thought in memory, some impressions strong, some weak, some lasting a length of time, some fading quickly.

We live our everyday lives on this surface, creating our dream picture of what is going on, maintaining ourselves rather precariously since there seems to be a limitless space above us and below us and nothing is permanent in the picture.

We seem somehow to be the sum total of our present impressions. Those impressions flooding in through the senses give us the sense that we are and we think that the world is separate from us and "out there".

What then would happen if the sensory impressions ceased?

It depends whether we think of them ceasing because we are asleep (we are "dead" to them) or because the body is dead.

Or whether we are able to withdraw *consciously* from the impressions.

If, through meditation, we could deliberately and consciously withdraw from the world of sense, where and what is that which is willing the withdrawal?

If I withdraw from sensory impressions, and then from mental thoughts and images, where am *I* and who am *I*?

Who is willing?

*

119

me

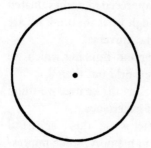 the world

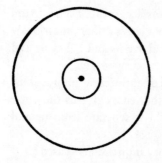 me in the world

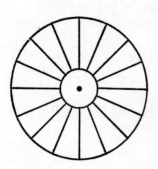 me, held in existence by the sphere of impressions coming from the world, subject to "the wheel of birth and death"

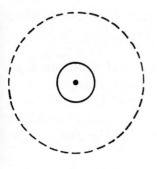

me withdrawn from the world
of sense impressions

"me" withdrawn; a dimensionless point or "all space";
no separation; no "other"

*

Gautama meditates . . . *or is said to do so.*
"Meditation", *in itself,* is "the mind in a state of meditation".
We can say: "That man is walking."
He *is* "walking". "Walking" is what he *is,* at the moment.
It is our description of his present form of action.
All such descriptions are of what a man is "doing".
But meditation is neither a describable activity of the mind nor
is it a particular posture, discipline or instruction (though these may
be helpful to enable meditation to "take place").
"Meditating" cannot be said to be "doing" anything.
Quite the opposite.
"Doing" ceases in meditation.
If there is "doing" then that is not meditation.
The motive, in meditation, is to withdraw from motive.
The only mental activity in meditation is to withdraw from
mental activity.
To *give up.*

In these religious or philosophical terms it is not "thinking about"; it is not thinking about not thinking.

It is "to be without thoughts".

It is "becoming the medium", "the Way", and because the desire is to be desire-less, the will to activate the mind withdraws.

There is no "subject" left to "do" the meditation. There is no "object" of meditation because there is no "subject" to relate it to.

"There is a path to walk on, there is walking being done, but there is no traveller . . ."

"There is existence, there is experience of existence, but there is no existing entity . . ."

"There is meditation, there is meditating being done, but there is no meditator . . ."

Someone walking past Gautama sitting on the grass beneath the tree might well have said, "Gautama is meditating".

But, to himself, in meditation, "Gautama" no longer existed.

*

For the sake of our attempt to describe what we have already established to be virtually indescribable, Gautama could be said to have left the world of phenomena and, by "withdrawal from" or "penetration through" layer after layer of passing experience, to have "reached" the realm of the formless, "the deathless state".

But "he" did not "get there".

It was only after what he might have described as total annihilation of himself, a kind of "conscious suicide", that there was the experience which he afterwards called *nirvana*—a timeless and dimensionless state of absolute "consciousness-knowledge-bliss".

This is extremely elusive for the logical mind which wants to say: "If there was an experience, there must have been someone to experience it."

Such is the limit of trying to describe the inexpressible.

We could suggest that there is a certain parallel to (and in a way, a complete fulfilment of) the state of the innocent baby—experiencing the world but not thinking itself as separate from the world nor the experience as happening to it. The consciousness-knowledge-bliss is not *by* anyone nor *of* anything. There is no subject, object nor relationship. It is pure consciousness itself, pure knowledge itself, pure bliss itself; so the subject and the object are *one* in consciousness, *one* in knowledge, *one* in bliss.

*

Gautama ceases to think of "himself" or for "himself", and is therefore not separate. He is in total sympathy.

In what respect are we truly separate from anything?

We only say we are so, in respect of objects which we wish to describe, to put "circles" round, so that we may relate them to ourselves and others. (Relate: meaning both "tell" *and* "the connection between one thing and another".) We put the circles round, circumscribe and therefore limit them, and we project them as objects; and then we believe them to be separate from us. Finally we like or dislike one thing in relation to another.

You may think and believe yourself separate from the page in front of you and you maybe liking or disliking its effect on you. But the separation is only an assumed belief established in memory as a result of many years of trying to find the relationship of things to yourself—*as your body*.

But look at this page—or touch it.

Where is it?

Is it "out there", in reality? Or is the sensory impression of the page in your mind?

Where is your mind?

What is "inside" your mind as opposed to "outside" it?

How large or small is your mind?

Is your mind (as distinct from what may happen to be "in" it) moving or still?

Everything is in mind.

Where else can it be?

And this page—these words on the page—are neutral. As you interpret the meaning, you may agree or disagree, like or dislike.

The mental disturbance comes between "you" and the "page"—and separates "you" from the "page".

Which is more relevant—to like or dislike what is written or to understand why you like or dislike it?

We place the praise or the blame on the "object out there"; rather less do we contemplate why we are praising or blaming; we rarely pause to consider what the liking or disliking is telling us about ourselves.

*

In his meditation, Gautama experiences what we might call "doubt".

In the story as handed down to us, he is visited by the god Mara, called in some translations, perhaps unexpectedly, the "God of Love". Mara tries to loosen Gautama's resolve to reach "the deathless state".

(Again, there is a significant parallel in this episode with the Christian story of Jesus's temptation in the wilderness by the devil who tempts him to take all worldly powers to himself.)

If we may focus on the title "God of Love" we may suggest an interpretation—presuming to put ourselves, within the limits of our own experience, into the situation of Gautama's difficulty.

"Love" suggests, in this context, attachment to the world's temptations. It means love for anything particular in the world, no matter how seemingly noble and worthwhile.

As we suggested earlier, the search for Truth is uncompromising in its total demand and is not an easy path.

Would we not have doubt if we were expected to surrender all such love?

Would we not be tempted to cling to what we believe in, respect, admire and worship?

How much do we depend on attachment to the world's ideas and ways for our sense of purpose, fulfilment, contentment, happiness and security?

Gautama is not only determined but well knows that such

attachment is reliance on the transitory, an illusion of love which is bound to decay and die. Through the experience of his "former lives"—of his life in the palace and his rigorous attachment to the mendicant's life—he knows that such possessive love makes demands and is full of the desires which bring in their aftermath despair and disappointment, depression and illness, because such attachment does not bring liberation. He knows that such love has hate as its compliment. It is not the real meaning of Love which knows no attachment, makes no demands, does not set up like against dislike, cannot repulse as it attracts, makes no preferences, which eliminates the illusion of duality, which is not exclusive but all-embracing and all-consuming, constant and compassionate . . . total sympathy.

*

I have severed all ties because I seek deliverance. How is it possible for me to return to the world? He who seeks religious truth, which is the highest treasure of all, must leave behind all that can concern him or draw away his attention, and must be bent upon that one goal alone. He must free his soul from covetousness and lust, and also from the desire for power.

Indulge in lust but a little, and lust like a child will grow. Wield worldly power and you will be burdened with cares. Better than sovereignty over the earth, better than living in heaven, better than lordship over all the worlds, is the fruit of holiness. I have recognized the illusory nature of wealth and will not take poison as food. Will a fish that has been baited still covet the hook, or an escaped bird love the net? Would a rabbit rescued from the serpent's mouth go back to be devoured? The sick man suffering from fever seeks a cooling medicine. Shall we advise him to drink that which will increase the fever? Shall we quench a fire by heaping fuel on it?

(*Sayings of Buddha*)

*

Gautama is not afraid of losing that which he once relied on but now knows to be deluding.

He presses on to the Ultimate.

This means losing all sense of himself as Gautama.

No clinging to thoughts of this nor thoughts of that.

To himself no longer located, he is no more.

Neither here nor there; neither everywhere nor nowhere; neither existing nor not-existing.

No word. No concept. No form. No entity.

No duality. Not a case of reconciling one with its opposite. Simply no experience of opposites. Only one. No opposition.

No time. No space. No separation.

No Gautama.

Gautama is no longer conceived of; is not now born; has ceased to become; cannot die.

Gautama is no longer Gautama . . .

only . . .

Buddha.

*

"The great seer, free from the dust of passion, victorious over darkness's gloom, has vanquished Mara. And the moon, like a maiden's gentle smile, lit up the heavens, while a rain of sweet-scented flowers, filled with moisture, fell down on the earth from above."

*

Buddha realization.

A clear state of mind, free from delusion, craving and aversion.

Buddha sees "his former lives": "There was I so and so; that was my name; deceased from there I came here."

Full of compassion, Buddha sees that all living things must ever move and change and may never rest in a sense of permanence in this world.

"Surely this world is unprotected and helpless, and like a wheel it turns round and round."

Buddha sees that the dis-ease and re-birth of beings depend on attachment to deeds and that no security may be found in *samsara*.

126

There is nothing stable, constant and substantial in the world of becoming.

*

"Alas, living beings wear themselves out in vain! Over and over again they are born, they age, die, pass on to a new life, and are reborn: What is more, greed and dark delusion obscure their sight, and they are blind from birth. Greatly apprehensive, they yet do not know how to get out of this great mass of ill."

*

Buddha sees that it is ignorance which binds men to illusion and which leads them to death. When ignorance is removed through contemplation, meditation and knowledge, the resulting disillusion liberates. The forming of *karma* gradually ceases and the illusion of an actual and permanent self dissolves.

*

It is recounted that:
"From the summit of the world downwards he could detect no self anywhere. Like the fire, when its fuel is burnt up, he became tranquil. He had reached perfection, and he thought to himself: 'This is the authentic Way on which in the past so many great seers, who also knew all higher and lower things, have travelled on to the ultimate and real truth . . .' "

*

Perhaps as we read of these events and hear the words of conviction, we feel a little sceptical, or fearful, or inadequate, or dismayed or in awe, or moved and inspired.

As we see how directly applicable the Gautama Buddha story is, at least in its early stages, to our own experience and questions, we are undoubtedly faced with a challenge.

We cannot deny, if we are prepared to admit it, that his observation of the human predicament is penetratingly accurate.

127

We can only ignore or accept the challenge.

If he "started off" with our questions and with our experiences and, through his determination he won through to "the further, the unbounded shore of *samsara*" . . . then *so may we*.

That will depend on the desire for Truth within us.

*

As we look at our present situation, "how we came to be here now", we can either press on regardless and hope that we shall find lasting happiness through our efforts in the world's terms or we may pause and contemplate where we are headed and whether the results we aspire to are likely to provide the benefit we expect and whether such benefit is what we really want.

At any moment, now, we can take stock of our experience and see if we are prepared to admit the unreliability and falseness of our beliefs.

It is not then a case of changing the world to suit our ideas of perfection. It need not necessarily mean changing the course of our own lives. It is simply a case of being prepared to admit how we have deluded ourselves in our expectations. It is our attitudes and beliefs that need to be honestly scrutinized. We suffer only because of them; ultimately there is no sense in blaming anyone or anything else. If we are discontented, fearful and frustrated because our desires are difficult to fulfil, should we not rather look at the validity of the desires and why we hold them than struggle with and cavil against the failure of the world to fulfil them?

If we see the illusion of what we expect of them, do we wish to cling to that illusion or are we prepared to accept disillusionment? Are we able to "turn round" and accept the possibility that pursuit of the world's temptations will bring no lasting happiness? Is it possible that the search for truth in the world's terms is doomed to failure? Is it reasonable that "the Way" to Truth is not a case of believing but of giving up false belief, and ultimately, belief itself?

Will we ever find the tranquil centre by going round and round the circumference? The repeating cycles of history tell us that mistakes are never rectified in an imaginary future; mistakes can only be rectified by the realization of them, and the decision not to repeat them, NOW.

The Buddha-state is not just something that happened to a man many centuries ago. It is always, NOW.

"But," protests the bewildered mind, "what will happen to me if I surrender my desires and beliefs?"

Liberation!

*

To come to the tranquil centre we have simply to be without thoughts.

Being without thoughts is the secret of meditation.

Meditation is not something you learn to do.

You may learn a technique *of* meditating, and with the aid of a technique you may gradually learn to disassociate yourself from the innumerable and constant thoughts circling in mind—but this is not meditation, it is still the technique.

As breath is to the body, so meditation is to the spirit.

When the mind is still, tranquil, serene, then there is total sympathy.

When the mind is still, tranquil, serene, then there is only Meditation.

Meditation is not something that you acquire or some state that you reach for.

Meditation is the constant breath of the spirit which is always here, NOW.

Through whatever technique you choose to employ you dis-cover that which has always been present.

"The still centre of the turning world."

*

Not Gautama, not you, not me, but:

"Buddha thought: 'Here I have found freedom.' And he knew that the longings of his heart had at last come to fulfilment. Now that he had grasped the principle of causation, and finally convinced himself of the lack of self in all that, he roused himself again from his deep trance, and in his great compassion he surveyed the world with his Buddha-eye, intent on giving it peace."

Eight

There were once two writers who came together to collaborate on a book.

The subject of the book was The Buddha Way *and the object of the book was to discover through the process of writing it, all that they could about the life and teachings of Siddhartha Gautama, in their own experience.*

They worked diligently and found out many things about themselves and about each other, but always they questioned whether they were expressing the Buddha Way.

"How can you express the inexpressible?" one of them would ask.

"It is not possible," the other would agree.

"All that we are doing," one would say, "is filling empty pages with many words."

"All that we desire," the other would continue, "is the empty page."

But you cannot write without words; you cannot have a book without words; and this was their dilemma. For their discoveries led them to the conviction that the only way to a sympathetic union with Gautama was through a silent, serene mind—empty of all words, all ideas, all thoughts.

"We are writing this book to be read," one of them said.

"And to be understood," the other one said.

"By whom?" the first enquired.

"Not only by some unknown reader," the second replied, "but by each of us."

What do we understand, having written so far this book called The Buddha Way?

"What did Gautama understand about the Buddha Way?"

They were silent for a moment, and between them, as they faced each other across the table, was a silence that contained them: The silence "inside" them, the silence "outside" them; no "inside", no "outside".

Silence.

And, in that moment, there was Knowledge that they were Gautama and understood only as Gautama understood.

Who writes this book?

Why is it written?

Who reads this book?

Why will they read it?

Could it have been written in any other way than the way that it is? If it had been—it would not be this book.

Can the reader understand it or not understand it in any other way?

What the readers make of it is their personal experience.

They will accept it or reject it.

That is their experience.

The writer is the reader—he reads "what is written", and interprets.

The reader is the writer—he reads "what is written", and interprets.

But if the mind is serene and silent:

There is a book to write, there is writing being done, but there is no writer . . .

There is a book to read, there is reading being done, but there is no reader . . .

The paradox dissolves in the empty, silent mind.

"There is a book being written," they said, and they each picked up their pens.

*

Enlightenment.

To see in a different way.

To have revealed that which was obscured.

To have the weight of difficulty and anxiety removed.

To have that which was dark and problematic illuminated and clear.

To comprehend that which had hitherto been ignored.

By the power of consciousness . . . by the miracle of understanding . . . by the certainty of innate knowledge . . . by the virtue of experience . . . by the sympathy of recognition . . . by the serenity of silent listening . . . that which was ignored is made evident.

And as opposed to the limiting bondage of belief and opinion based on indiscriminate learning—a kind of adopted, makeshift and partial truth—there is liberating conviction in that which is undeniable.

Once illusion is seen, it is hard to maintain belief in it. He who is prepared to do so admits the disillusionment.

The ultimate disillusionment is that there never was, never is and never will be a permanent, phenomenal self.

*

Would an "author" write a "bad" book?

Should he set out to do so, he will write a "good" bad book!

All the judgements of the world are based on the belief in a permanent, phenomenal self.

The basest actions known to mankind are enacted because the the activator couldn't—at that moment—do anything else. And yet we judge a man by his actions. We rarely ask, "Who is acting?" or "Why?"

Do we chide a tree for growing a crooked branch? The shape of the branch is dictated by its effort to reach the light.

Do we chide an animal for behaving contrary to our desire? It is behaving true to its nature.

We may train the branch, we may train the animal—but we will always be limited by its nature.

A tree will not grow in the dark; a dog will not live under water.

And of course, we would not want them to.

Yet we would have the world altered to suit our convenience.

We judge the world to suit our convenience.

But do any of us know our true convenience?

We, the authors, are not excusing our book to you, the reader.

133

Rather we are as much in the dark as you. What light there may be is not "ours" to give to "you".

If there is "light", it is "in the light of experience".

There is no "wrong" or "right".

There is only "enlightenment".

"Enlightenment" does not belong to Gautama, or to you or to me.

"Enlightenment" does not "belong to".

Enlightenment is.

There never was, never is and never will be a permanent phenomenal self.

This kind of realization rarely comes of its own accord. It has to to be sought and worked for, by those who are moved to do so, through discrimination (through the evaluating organ of mind called *buddhi*) by distinguishing the real and reliable from the false and shifting.

And this will hardly be done while the mind chases unceasingly from one thing to the next, seeking pleasure, avoiding pain. It can only be done when there is a pause or interval, a conscious observation of what is going on, a standing back from the activity, a withdrawal from the chase.

Only in the mind clear of craving and aversion is there the state of meditation.

*

Certainly this process is neither easy nor comfortable because it means total self-surrender. It means abandonment of trust in the explanations, values and authorities of the world. It is a kind of living, conscious "suicide".

But, when the idea and assumption and belief of self has gone, there is nothing left to die, except the body.

*

Gautama determines to discover "the deathless state".

He sits down to meditate.

Gautama merges into Buddha . . . and except as a physical human

134

body, named "Gautama", Gautama no longer exists to himself.

So it becomes for us if we are drawn along the Buddha Way.

We become no longer what we have thought that we were.

We may also merge into Buddha . . . when we no longer believe and act as though we are anyone else.

Gautama is said to have been in meditation under the tree for forty-nine days.

We can, if we wish, in the world's terms take that to mean seven weeks of historical duration. Or, we may, if we wish, suspect that it is symbolic ("day" having the connotations of light representing consciousness, as opposed to the "darkness" of night, and forty-nine having mystical significance as seven times seven).

The choice is up to us, according to what it suits us to believe.

But for Gautama himself?

For Buddha meditating . . . no time at all.

From the Buddha point of view . . . in the deathless state of deep meditation . . . no past, no future, no time . . . only timeless NOW.

NOW . . . as unconditioned, pure consciousness . . . is all that there really *is*, ever.

*

But whilst the body remains, there is continuing.

Let us consider the historical record of the Gautama story a little further.

After he had realized the *dharma*—a total, all embracing, unifying truth concerning all things at whatever level of expression, all-at-once—Gautama's mind is flooded with enlightenment.

He has gone from the world. No motivation remains. *Nirvana*.

Absolute consciousness-knowledge-bliss. No self-consciousness.

Why come back?

Gautama's body is still there under the tree.

The existence draws consciousness back to itself.

Gautama "returns" to exist again to himself.

How to continue in the world?

At first his mind is filled with sympathy as he sees the world, as

135

if for the first time, and through the sympathy comes the serenity of compassion and the resolve to give to the world the peace that he has found. But then he considers the ways of the world and bondage of man to craving and aversion and he is daunted by the thought that men will never accept his analysis of the causes of "ill-state", will never comprehend the subtlety and the sacrifice of the Way, will not dare to face the implications of surrendering all for Truth.

But then he reflects that though the majority will pay him no heed because of their commitment to the pursuit of happiness in the world, there will surely be some who will be prepared to listen to him. There will be some whose longing for Truth, no matter how weak or strong, will respond to whatever help and guidance he can give.

Such reflections, combined with his recollection of his early vows to help his fellow men, finally restores his resolve to return to his body, his earthly existence, to the world, in order to teach those who will listen.

And this he does for the remaining historical duration of his body —forty-five years.

*

This is sacrifice indeed.

Buddha does not need to return.

Indeed for Buddha there is no "re-turning", there is no "here" and "there".

But the body is still "there" . . . to be of service.

When self-motivation has ceased, the mind directs the body solely for the purpose of being of service to others, of helping them.

But only for the purpose of helping them to understand Truth . . . not helping them to find transitory comfort and security in the world.

*

Those foolish people who torment themselves, as well as those who have become attached to the domains of the senses, both these should be viewed as faulty in their method, because they are not on the way to

136

deathlessness. These so-called austerities but confuse the mind which is overpowered by the body's exhaustion. In the resulting stupor one can no longer understand the ordinary things of life, how much less the way to the Truth which lies beyond the senses. The minds of those, on the other hand, who are attached to the worthless sense-objects, are overwhelmed by passion and darkening delusion. They lose even the ability to understand the doctrinal treatises, still less can they succeed with the method which by suppressing the passions leads to dispassion. So I have given up both these extremes, and have found another path, a middle way. It leads to the appeasing of all ill, and yet it is free from happiness and joy.

*

In this expression "middle way" we have the subtlest of knife-edge paths to follow.

For the simple—but profoundly subtle and extremely hard—principle of the Middle Way is that anything said or done through *selfish motivation*, no matter how good and noble in the world's eyes, is bondage to illusion and will not lead to the deathless state. To be able to discriminate between selfish and not-selfish requires constant patience and perseverance.

Why?

Because self-motivation is based on belief in "me". And "my" desires and fears are legion. Born into the samsaric world of existence, the mind learns to serve "me" and "mine". The mind is heavily committed to the security and survival of "me". It becomes almost totally enslaved by the karmic view—cause and effect, sequence and consequence. In believing in "me", the mind creates a fictional, shifting, ephemeral entity, supposedly independent and separate from the world, whose only goal is death.

There is no compromise with this state; and yet the mind is loth to surrender it.

Hence the difficulty of the Middle Way.

For the mind wants salvation, liberation, eternal life, truth or whatever, for "*me*".

And herein lies the subtlety . . . and the need for year upon year of patience and perseverance to accomplish "conscious suicide".

For, paradoxically, there is no such thing as liberation *for* the self; the Way leads to liberation *from* the self.

*

It is not a case of me becoming perfect, me serving my fellow men, me serving "God", me suffering for the sake of others. That is all delusion (though, we might add, a more healthy and wholesome state than my harming or exploiting in response to the lust for power and possession).

All "me" has to be surrendered . . . the supposedly "good" me as well as the supposedly "bad". The me that performs altruistic and saintly deeds in my estimation and in worldly terms in order to win reward and salvation in some "other" life is as illusory as the me who "sins". It is all delusion of the mind.

And yet, ironically and paradoxically, it is the very delusion of liberation and salvation for "me" that will first set each of us on the quest for "the deathless state".

The Middle Way is unrelenting. If we start off giving up that which is supposedly "bad" then we will inevitably be led to a point where there is no "good". "Good" is only held in place by illusion of "bad". The illusion in mind is held there by "me".

All that has to be surrendered is "me".

Who does the surrendering?

I do.

How can I give up being me?

The "I" sees the suffering, decay, aging and death of me.

The "I" sees the suffering, decay, aging and death of all things.

Who am I?

Buddha.

How can I ever know that I am Buddha?

I cannot . . . Buddha knows.

In the deluded and distracted mind, pursuing desire and avoiding pain, Buddha suffers as the self in each and every human being.

138

In the clear and meditating mind, the self dissolves and Buddha suffers the world to be.

*

Words fall short, especially written ones.

Which, we may presume, is why Gautama, and all men of such stature and understanding, never wrote anything down and only responded orally, appropriately to the audience and circumstance of any moment, NOW.

A question, for example, is never as important as *how* and *why* it is being asked—and that can only be taken into account when face to face with the questioner.

Nevertheless, we may deduce a great deal from recorded testimony, especially if we find our minds responding to it because it confirms our own experience and intuition. It does not matter if we have not got it "right" because it would only be "not right" in someone else's opinion. We may well take note of their opinion to see if it helps in any way, but the really important factor is whether we *know* it is helping us *at the time*. That is what counts.

There is an old saying:

"You take a thorn to remove a thorn—and then you throw them both away."

So it is with the Middle Way.

Only I know that I have a thorn sticking into me. You may say, "Why prod yourself with a thorn—that is absurd!"

Gautama Buddha's teaching is in essence very simple. The difficulty is putting it into practice.

He does not ask that a man should believe anything that he is not able to experience and discover for himself "in this life". (In this sense, belief should not be confused with faith. It could be said that faith is what is left when all belief has been surrendered.)

He does not propose a "God", a "soul", an identifiable, reincarnating "self"; rather does he say that all such concepts and forms are man-created and illusory. To commit the mind to belief in such fictions is delusion.

Why believe in such concepts?

Something is proposed and then believed in response to a lacking, and thence a desire, in mind. We make things up and then explain and try to prove them because we think we need a structure of belief to rely on. What sense is there in that?

Gautama Buddha proposes that man's salvation is up to man himself and that he has the capacity within him to accomplish it. It is no good looking elsewhere for it. The necessary knowledge is within each individual, not in the propositions and concepts of others. Each individual—you and me—takes a step on the Buddha Way each time he works something out and realizes in his own experience *for himself*.

Thus the Way has nothing to do with committing to belief; rather is it the conscious dispelling of false belief.

When all make-believe has been removed, only faith remains . . . not faith *in* anything . . . just faith . . . a total, selfless, unifying *with* everything.

And we have such glimpses of faith when we sense something of "breathtaking" beauty. In the exquisite scent of a flower we may for a moment experience the ecstasy of complete and selfless surrender. Total sympathy. Bliss.

*

At first, much that we have been saying above may not seem to have anything to do with religion. In fact, some may even seem anti-religious, agnostic or atheistic; and, in a superficial sense that would be a valid assessment. It tends to appear so because it seems to run counter to the ideas about religion commonly taught and learned in religious establishments. The commonest impression of the meaning of religion is that we should believe there to be an Almighty Power—named God, Jehovah, Allah, Brahman, or whatever—to whom we humans are subject and whom we should obey, worship, praise, and so forth.

But these are only the names used in different forms of religion to denote the transcendent Principle of the Universe. This Principle and its Laws govern every atom of energy-matter and every form taken by that energy-matter, including the human form. The unique capacity of the human mind is to comprehend that Principle. All human activity as dictated by it and Man has a choice; either he remains subject to it and ignorant of it, in which case all his endeavour is ultimately pointless and meaningless; or he becomes conscious of it, in which case he becomes naturally obedient to its Laws and aspires to merge with and become the Principle. The Principle is represented in Man by the symbol and sense of "I".

"Who am I?" is the Principle "re-calling" itSelf. It is through man aspiring to and consciously merging with the One Principle that the Principle becomes conscious of itSelf. Working towards that Principle is being religious and the method by which it is to be accomplished constitutes the character and form of a particular religion.

Thus, in all forms of religion, the purpose and fulfilment of human life is to discover and surrender to the ultimate Principle so that it may be experienced. In each case this requires abandonment of self-will (which in effect is thinking and assuming that one may act autonomously) and this requires in its preparatory stages help and discipline.

Buddhism, in this context, is undoubtedly "a religion"; it differs from other forms of religion only in its emphasis and method. It does not formalize and name the Principle, thereby avoiding the problems that arise from the temptation to describe, formulate, attribute to, locate, characterize, personalize, and objectify the Principle. (It is for this reason that Buddhism at first seems impersonal, calculating, atheistic, unemotional, and so on.) Rather it lays emphasis on observation and realization of the fiction of self (and the suffering and ill-state resulting from its maintenance) so that only by discrimination the individual willingly and naturally withdraws to fulfilment in the unnamed and unconditioned Principle. This we may call aspiring to knowledge and experience of "God", providing there is absolutely no concept in the mind of what the word "God" means.

*

Due to subsequent interpretation, in the world's terms, it is frequently thought that Buddhism is synonymous with self-denial in a very literal sense so that the penniless mendicant or monk with begging bowl, shaven head and yellow robes has become identified as typical representation of a particular form of religion.

But this is surely nonsense.

This is only performance of a form of religion; being religious does not need outward show; quite the contrary. (Certainly rituals and vestments can exert a hypnotic power, generate a sense of occasion and command discipline, as they do in say, the armed forces; but the danger is that the performance becomes an end in itself, which has nothing to do with religion. But, again, let us be wary of making judgements beyond *our own* experience! Who can say what *any* "outward show" means to the person we are observing? Are we even aware of our own "outward show"? If we were to be challenged, then perhaps we could "explain" it—or, perhaps, we are unaware of it. We are always only *being* what we are at that particular moment. It depends upon the "honesty" of the individual. And no person can be honest for us; we cannot be honest for any other person.)

The spirit of Buddhism essentially has nothing to do with literal performance of self-mortification. It does not mean giving up the world literally. (But if the only way for a particular individual to discover this for himself requires him to attempt such mortification and denial then I should not judge him, nor should he despair. After all, such an Individual is treading a similar path to Gautama. The essence is meeting the disillusion when it arises and being undeterred in the singular aim.) Buddhism has nothing to do with worshipping gods; nothing to do with superstitious subjection to hypothetical powers.

Basically it only requires a reasonable, sensible, practical assessment of human existence and the exercise of the power of discrimination, asking only that the individual should learn from his experience.

Let us NOW, each of us—we the writers and you the reader—

give up judging another man's behaviour (however "absurd" it may seem to each of us). Which of us can say *why* another man behaves as he does?

"*Be ye lamps unto yourselves . . .*"

*

After enlightenment, Gautama outlined for the *guidance* of others the basic situation. This discourse has become known as The Four Noble Truths. These four are sometimes called:

Holy Truth of Ill.
Holy Truth of Origination of Ill.
Holy Truth of the Stopping of Ill.
Holy Truth as to the Method of Stopping of Ill.

In short, these Four Truths state that born into *samsara*, we find ourselves in a state of insecurity. Because of this state of anxiety we seek relief by desiring to find satisfaction in the world. But the things of the world are in themselves impermanent; therefore our craving meets with disappointment and we suffer. This suffering can only be stopped by ceasing the craving for, and the aversion to, the things of the world. This means withdrawal or non-attachment (*not* detachment). Or, as it has been put elsewhere, "being *in* the world, but not *of* it". This can only be done by a process of discrimination, or evaluation, renouncing the false and illusory, by following what Gautama called the Eightfold Path, which means the discipline of right view based on right understanding, right thought based on right intent, right speech, right conduct, right livelihood, right effort, right mindfulness or attention, right concentration.

He who *ignores* the Four Truths remains in *ignorance* and, in continuing to seek and pursue happiness in the world, renders himself subject to the wheel of birth-death, cause and effect, sequence and consequence.

It is simply a case of suffering or suffering to be.

*

Gradually the process of liberation takes place (though in moments of realization or enlightenment it may seem "sudden").

143

Indeed the process has already begun. But you cannot buy a "map" and say "I am here—and I have so far to go". It is not like that. Enlightenment is "so near and yet so far". We cannot be "nearly enlightened". There is only *Enlightenment*; all else is the *Way*.

Broadly speaking, the whole process may be seen as linked to understanding that all suffering and disturbance is due to selfish concern and its repercussions.

Any man is only what he thinks he is. And anything he thinks he is is subject to change, decay and death. Why believe such things? That thought-created self must slowly and surely dissolve.

Thus I may think myself "enlightened"; you may think yourself "enlightened". The history of mankind is littered with such deluded men.

Did Gautama "think himself enlightened"?

There is no Gautama in the enlightened state.

Buddha enlightens Buddha.

As the self dissolves, the reality dawns and final liberation from the self—full enlightenment—is Buddha-realization, *nirvana*.

The being, free of self-concern, is then available to serve the appropriate need as long as the body remains.

*

No teacher have I. None need I venerate, and none must I despise. Nirvana have I now obtained, and I am not the same as others. Quite by myself, you see, have I the Dharma won. Completely have I understood what must be understood, though others failed to understand it. That is the reason why I am Buddha. The hostile forces of defilement I have vanquished. That is the reason why I should be known as one whose self is calmed. And, having calmed myself, I now am on my way to Varanasi, to work the weal of fellow-beings still oppressed by many ills. There shall I beat the deathless Dharma's drum, unmoved by pride, not tempted by renown. Having myself crossed the ocean of suffering, I must help others to cross it. Freed myself, I must set others free. This is the vow which I made in the past when I saw all that lives in distress.

*

Who am I?
... *I am Buddha* ...

*

The unconditioned Self, the "I", the ultimate Principle, is both the centre, the circumference and the whole.

Withdrawn into itSelf, it is the deathless, formless, timeless, unborn, undying life or spirit which transmigrates from form to form—as a flame, itself unchanging, may be transferred from candle to candle. If it may be described as anything, it is absolute consciousness-knowledge-bliss.

Expressing itSelf, it is the care and compassion for the world, which once released from the "heart" spreads out to the limits of Mind as love in all its forms. In its limited forms such love is conditioned and becomes attached; in its unlimited expression it is not confined to particular form but serves unconditionally that need which is made known through the minds and bodies of the "religious".

*

Who is "religious"?

There are said to have been many Buddhas prior to Gautama, the most recent one. Buddhists are said to be waiting for the next Buddha, named Maitreya.

In historical, evolutionary terms, we may assume this to mean that one day such a man may appear as the culmination of a process of spiritual development which began in the distant past, many aeons ago.

Or, in terms of the timeless reality of here and now, Maitreya is that "I" in you and in me who may . . . suddenly . . . be revealed . . . as the being who remains when all untruth and false belief is abandoned.

At that point, the living centre . . .

there is only Meditation . . .

nothing else.

No longer
"Who am I?" . . .
No longer
"I" . . . seeking answers . . .
only "I" . . . meditating.

*

> Those who perform meditation for even one session
> Destroy innumerable accumulated sins;
> How should there be wrong paths for them?
> The Paradise of Buddha is not far.

(from HAKUNI's *The Song of Meditation*)

The perfect way knows no difficulties
Except that it refuses to make preferences;
Only when freed from hate and love
It reveals itself fully and without disguise;
A tenth of an inch's difference
And heaven and earth are set apart.
If you wish to see it before your own eyes
Have no fixed thoughts either for or against it . . .